LET'S PARTY! KIDS COOKBOOK

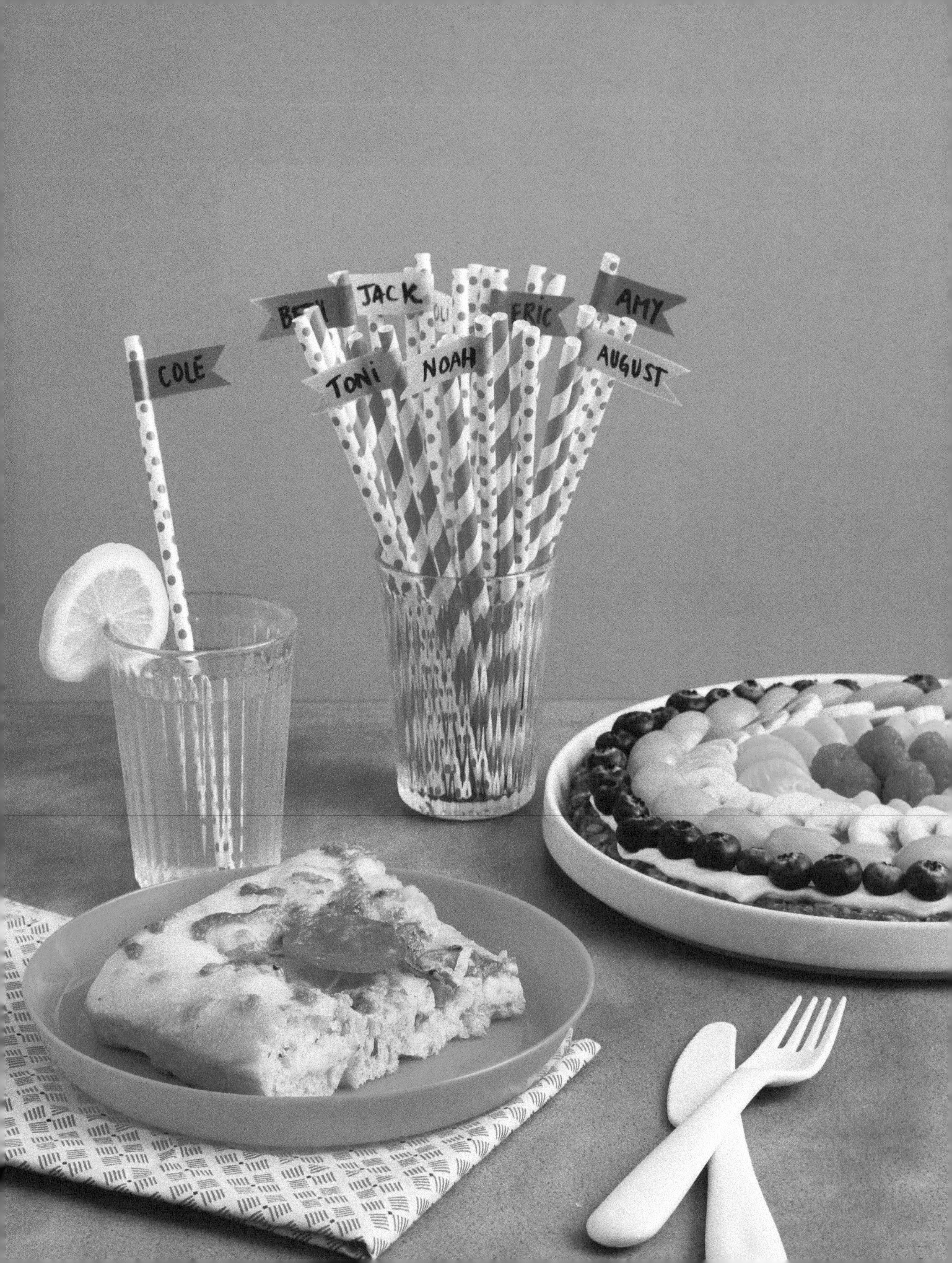
COLE
JACK
ERIC
AMY
TONI
NOAH
AUGUST

LET'S PARTY!
KIDS COOKBOOK

Tasty Recipes Kids Will Love to Make, Eat, and Share

By Ashley Moulton

ROCKRIDGE
PRESS

Interior and Cover Designer: Erin Yeung
Art Producer: Sue Bischofberger
Editor: Lauren Ladoceour
Production Editor: Jenna Dutton

Photography: © 2019 Laura Flippen, cover and pp. ii, vi, viii, 2–3, 15–17, 30–31, 41, 42–43, 52–53, 61, 62–63, 71, 72–73, 84–85, 93, 94–95, 104–105, 111, 114–115, 120, 124–125, 134–135, 143, 144–145, 155, 156; © Evi Abeler, pp. 18–19, 21, 78, and 131; © Helene Dujardin, pp. 25 and 101; © Melina Hammer, p. 44; © Nadine Greeff, p. 153.

ISBN: Print 978-1-64152-868-9 | eBook 978-1-64152-869-6

R0

For Daniel and Juniper: Here's to the many
things we will celebrate together.

CONTENTS

IT'S YOUR PARTY

Who doesn't love a party? It's an awesome way to hang out with your friends, make decorations, play games, and share your favorite foods until you're all partied out. This cookbook's got everything you need to plan ahead or take an everyday hangout with your pals and turn it into a celebration with tasty snacks you can make yourself. Whatever inspires you to get in the kitchen, cooking for friends and family is a heartfelt way to show them how much you care.

We'll start with everything you'll need to know to plan and cook for a party. No worries if you haven't cooked very much before. These recipes will help you learn!

After we've covered the basics, you'll get to pick what kind of party you want to throw. Each party chapter has a different theme, like "Superhero Party" or "Hawaiian Luau," and comes with a drink recipe, a delicious snack, and a dessert recipe. These chapters also include ideas for decorations and activities you can do with your guests. You can use this book lots of ways: Make all three recipes for a party, mix and match recipes from different parties, or just make one recipe when you're looking for something to do. As the chef and host, you're in charge!

A NOTE TO GROWN-UPS

Remember when your toddler used to play for hours with pots, pans, and a wooden spoon? Now that your child is growing up, they can actually start cooking—and make food for others. Kids feel a sense of pride and agency when they cook, and they delight in telling friends and family that they're responsible for the delicious snacks on offer. Cooking also teaches kids math and a little science.

This book is designed to help kids cook and share food with others for one of their favorite things: A PARTY! They'll learn kitchen skills, how to be a good host and care for guests, and new games to play with friends along the way. Most recipes, activities, and decorations make excellent rainy-day projects or boredom busters. Many include satisfying snacks and can be made with ingredients you likely already have at home. Others have make-ahead tips or are great for everyone at the party to make together.

Kids are impulsive, and they'll probably want to start sending invitations right away. So point them to the beginning chapters before they jump in. Chapter 1 is all about how to throw a party, and chapter 2 goes over basic cooking and baking skills they'll use. There are 12 party chapters, each with a different theme and three recipes (a drink, savory snack, and dessert), as well as decoration and activity ideas.

Recipes serve four to six people but can easily be doubled or tripled if there's a larger crowd. All recipes are labeled with allergen labels, and many include substitution ideas. You'll also find icons for the cooking skills taught in chapter 2, so you know exactly what you might need to help them with:

 MEASURING   OVEN

 MIXING   STOVETOP

 KNIVES

The recipes inside are what I like to call "healthy-ish." They are nutritionally balanced enough for everyday eating, but I believe that treats are a part of a good diet, too. They use whole, unprocessed ingredients when feasible and emphasize cooking from scratch. They limit sugar, as well, to avoid wired party guests.

Who is this book for? Any child age eight or older who wants to cook! No prior experience is necessary. You, the grown-up, should absolutely be around and available as a safety measure, and also look out for any recipe steps with a ✋ symbol next to it (that's you and your kid's cue they might need to call you over). Either way, you know your kid and what they can handle best, so you make the rules.

Just be sure to keep it fun. After all, parties are about imagination and play—whether that's a tea party with stuffed animals, a last-minute sleepover, or a half-birthday bash. Whatever the occasion, there will be plenty of yummy treats for kids to make, eat, and (most important) share.

PART ONE
Getting Started

CHAPTER 1
You're Invited

So you're ready to host a party? This is your official invitation to learn everything you need to know to throw the yummiest and most fun bash possible.

HOW TO THROW A PARTY

All you need to do to throw a great get-together with friends is follow the steps below. First, you'll plan your party, then you'll make what you need for the party, and then . . . you'll party!

Plan

1. **Find something to celebrate.** There are so many reasons to celebrate besides your birthday! It could be the last day of school, a snow day, or a plain old Saturday when you just need something fun to do. There's really no bad reason to throw a party.

2. **Pick a theme and recipes**. You can pick a party chapter from this book and make just one or all three recipes from the menu or mix and match recipes from other party chapters. You can even add your personal favorite recipes to the menu. You're the host, so you decide!

3. **Ask an adult for permission.** Ask a grown-up before you invite guests. Tell your grown-up what food you'd like to serve, when you'd like to have the party, and how many guests you'd like to have. Thumbs up? Invite away!

4. **Make a guest list and send out invites.** Let your guests know important party information, like when and where to show up.

5. **Make a grocery list.** Make a list of all the ingredients you need and see which ones you already have at home. If you need to buy some ingredients, ask your grown-up to add them to their shopping list or go to the supermarket with them!

Make

1. **Read through the recipes.** Before you get started, read through the recipes so you know how they work, if you have enough time to cook them, and the order you should cook them in. Also, look out for any recipe steps with a ✋ symbol next to it. You'll want to make sure there's an adult around who can help you with those.

2. **Wash your hands.** It's super important that you wash your hands before cooking, after using the bathroom, after you sneeze, or after working with raw eggs, meat, or fish. If you have long hair, it's a great idea to tie it back. Getting sick from germs is not a great party favor!

3. **Prepare your work area.** Clear the kitchen counters, take out the ingredients and equipment, and have the recipe close by. Wear an apron to protect your clothes and get a step stool if the counter is taller than your elbow.

4. **Rinse the produce.** Most fruits and veggies need to be washed before you start. Put all your produce in a colander and run water from the tap over it. Some things like cilantro or lettuce can be very sandy, so those should be dunked in a bowl of water. Delicate produce like herbs and lettuce should be dried with a clean kitchen towel or spun in a salad spinner.

5. **Use kitchen tools and appliances safely.** There are lots of times to be silly, but cooking is not one of them. Make sure you are very careful and pay close attention when you use knives, sharp appliances like blenders, and anything that heats food like the stovetop, oven, or microwave. And the number-one safety rule: Always have a grown-up nearby when you cook!

6. **Clean as you go.** One way to stay on top of the party prep mess is to do the dishes after each recipe or during downtime in a recipe (like when something is in the oven). It's especially important to clean right after you've used raw eggs or meat. In addition to washing your hands, wash cooking tools with hot soapy water and disinfect surfaces with an antibacterial cleaner.

7. **Set the table**. Set up your plates, silverware, cups, and napkins on the table or at the buffet. Spend a few minutes tidying the room and setting up decorations. Make sure there are enough chairs for your guests. Play your favorite playlist with a speaker to create the right mood.

Party

1. **Make guests feel welcome.** If your party spot is hard to find, you can hang a balloon or a sign to help guests know where to go. When guests arrive, ask if you can take their coat or umbrella and put it somewhere safe. Offer them something to drink and show them where the food and bathroom are located.

2. **Serve food.** You might have some appetizers and snacks already set up when guests arrive so they can help themselves. Decide what time you'd like to serve any main courses or dessert. It can be a good idea to set an alarm to remind yourself in case you're having too much fun! You'll need to gather your guests at the table or buffet when it's time to eat.

3. **Have fun!** Sometimes when you're a party host, you can get so busy that you forget to enjoy yourself. Make sure you remember to spend time enjoying the food you've made, playing games, and hanging out with your friends.

4. **Clean up.** The final party step is less fun but just as important. Return everything to the way you found it. Do the dishes, take down the decorations, put the furniture back, and take out the trash and recycling.

INGREDIENTS

The recipes in this book use a lot of different ingredients, but these are the ones you'll see the most. If you already have these at home, you can cook party food anytime!

In the Pantry

All-purpose flour
Baking chocolate
Baking powder
Baking soda
Brown sugar
Confectioner's sugar
Cornstarch
Garlic powder
Granulated sugar
Ground cinnamon

Ground cumin
Honey or maple syrup
Nonstick cooking spray
Oil (like olive, canola, sunflower, or avocado)
Pepper
Salt
Soda water
Vanilla extract
Whole-wheat flour

In the Fridge + Freezer

Eggs
Fresh fruit like blueberries
Fresh herbs like basil
Fresh vegetables like carrots
Frozen fruit like strawberries
Greek yogurt
Heavy whipping cream
Ice cubes

Lemons
Limes
Milk of choice
Oranges
Shredded, sliced, and blocked cheeses
Tortillas
Unsalted butter

On the Counter

Bananas
Beefsteak tomatoes
Cherry or grape tomatoes
Fruit that needs to ripen, like avocados and peaches

Garlic
Onions

KITCHEN EQUIPMENT

Get to know these cooking items because you'll use them most often for the recipes in this book.

Tools + Utensils

Oven mitts

Chef's knife

Cutting boards

Measuring cups
(dry and liquid)

Measuring spoons

Mixing bowls

Wooden spoon

Whisk

Fine-mesh strainer

Colander

Rolling pin

Pastry brush

Zester or
box grater

Potato masher

Cookie cutters

Spatulas

Cooling rack

Kitchen tongs

Vegetable peeler

Parchment paper,
plastic wrap,
aluminum foil

Cookware + Bakeware

Large stockpot

Rimmed
baking sheet

Skillet

Muffin pan and
cupcake liners

9-inch round
cake pans

Ramekins

Appliances

Blender or food processor

Electric hand mixer or stand mixer

Microwave

Oven

BE MY GUEST

It would be great if you could invite 100 of your favorite people to every party you throw, but that would be way too much work! If you aren't able to invite everyone you'd like to and you're worried about hurting someone's feelings, try saying, "I'm so sorry I couldn't invite you this time, but let's make a plan to hang out soon!"

Another great thing about parties? Guests don't have to come from outside of your house. You could be home on a rainy day, and your guests could be stuffed animals, pets, or a family member. Even the food, decorations, and party activities can be made from things you already have in the house.

If you're planning a party ahead of time, you'll need to send an invite by text message, phone call, email, online invitation, or a paper card. Your invite should include:

* Date and time of the party

* Address of the party

* Party theme

* Any items guests should bring

* RSVP date and how to contact you

Why include an RSVP? RSVP comes from the French phrase *répondez s'il vous plaît*, which means "please respond." When you know how many people are coming, you can make sure you have enough food and games for everyone. This is a good opportunity to ask your buddies if they have any allergies or don't eat meat, so you can plan a menu they'll enjoy.

JOIN ME FOR A PARTY!

Why: Just for fun!

Date: June 15th

Time: 12:00 p.m.

Where: My backyard

Bring: A game to play

RSVP to me by June 12th

(555) 555-5555

SERVE WARE

When you throw a party, you want to make it look nice! Serve ware, or special plates and tools that help you serve food, will help you present your food in a festive way. Reusable glasses, plates, silverware, napkins, and tablecloths are great, but if you're feeding a large crowd, it may be more convenient to use disposable items. You might even live in a place where plastic disposables are recyclable and paper plates are compostable. These items will help your food look as good as it tastes.

SET THE STAGE

Buffet or sit-down? It's up to you! Buffet (pronounced "buh-*fay*") parties are when you set up food on serving platters and let guests serve themselves. Sit-down parties are when guests sit around a table and you bring the food to them.

Buffets are great when you have a lot of guests or when your meal includes a lot of toppings, like Splendid Sundaes (page 99). Also, buffets are perfect when food is meant to be part of the decoration, like in the Halloween Boo-ffet (page 135). Just make sure you have serving dishes (like large bowls, platters, a cake stand) and serving utensils (like large spoons, tongs, or a pie cutter) for each dish. For a special drink, a large pitcher is handy. Set up a stack of plates at one end of the buffet table and napkins, utensils, and cups at the other end. Flowers are always a nice touch, no matter the occasion.

Sit-down parties are an awesome way for a small number of guests to laugh and talk around a table—or if you want your party to feel fancier. Parties from this book that would work well as a sit-down style include the Tea Party (page 63) and the Pizza Party (page 73). Set up a place setting (plate, fork, knife, spoon, napkin, glass) in front of each chair at the table. You'll probably need serving plates and utensils for each dish you bring out, so your friends can pass the food around and help themselves.

A Fork		**D** Plate	
B Knife and spoon		**E** Cups	
C Napkin		**F** Placemat	

G	Teapot and teacups	K	Serving spoons
H	Paper straws	L	Ladle
I	Drink pitcher	M	Serving platters
J	Serving bowls	N	Ice cream scoop

O	Tongs		S	Small plates
P	Pizza cutter		T	Cake stand
Q	Pie cutter		U	Toothpicks
R	Ice bowl		V	Centerpiece

CHAPTER 2
Kitchen Basics

Before you cook for a party, there are a few chef skills to learn. It's important to know how to read a recipe, how to measure, how to mix, and how to use the stovetop and oven. After you learn these skills, you'll be all set to cook for—and impress—your guests!

READING A RECIPE

You're excited to get cooking (and partying!), but it's important to read the whole recipe first. Start at the very top so you can triple check that:

- You have enough time to make the recipe

- You have all the ingredients for the right number of guests

- You have the right kitchen equipment

Then read through the recipe's instructions from start to finish. This will help you understand how all the ingredients are combined and keep you from making mistakes! Make a note in your head if any ingredients in the ingredient list say "divided." That means you'll use part of that ingredient in one recipe step and another portion of that ingredient in another step.

MEASURING

Measuring is a very important skill that will help your food taste great. Especially when you're baking something, it is super important to measure carefully. Baking is really just a yummy chemistry experiment; if you measure incorrectly, your dessert might not turn out quite right.

If the recipe is not a baked treat like cookies, cakes, or pancakes, your measurements don't have to be as exact. Sometimes a recipe will tell you to add something "to taste," which means you decide how much you put in depending on what tastes good to you.

Dry Measuring

To start, use measuring cups or spoons designed for measuring dry ingredients. They have numbers marked on the handles. Use the cup or spoon to scoop your ingredient and fill it so there's a heaping mound.

Then make it completely level: For a measuring cup, run the flat edge of a butter knife over the top edge of the measuring cup. For a measuring spoon, you can use your finger instead. Do the leveling over the ingredient's container so you don't waste the extra.

Liquid Measuring

When you're measuring liquids more than ¼ cup, make sure you use a liquid measuring cup (they're usually see-through and have numbers printed on the side). First, find the line for the amount the recipe calls for. Bend over so your eyes are even with that line. Pour the liquid until it reaches the top of the line. There usually will be a clear stripe at the top of your liquid; scientists call this the *meniscus*. You want the meniscus to be above the measurement line.

For liquids in smaller amounts like teaspoons or tablespoons, it's okay to use measuring spoons as long as you fill them to the top.

MAKING MORE OR LESS

What if you have more or fewer guests than your recipe makes?
  Let's say the recipe serves four people. If you have between five and eight guests coming, you'll want to double the recipe by multiplying each ingredient amount by two. So, 1 cup becomes 2, ¾ teaspoon becomes 1½ teaspoons, and so on. If you have between nine and a dozen people coming, you'll multiply the ingredient amounts by three instead (making 3 cups and 2¼ teaspoons in this example).
  What if you need to make less? Let's say the recipe makes a dozen cupcakes, but you have only six party guests. You'll need to cut every ingredient in half by dividing amounts by two. So ⅔ cup becomes ⅓ cup, and 2 teaspoons becomes 1 teaspoon.
  Helpful hints:

* Do the math before you start cooking and write down the new quantities for each ingredient.

* For help, use the conversions table (page 157).

* If you get stuck, grab a calculator.

MIXING

Mixing ingredients is easy if you follow the recipe's directions. Pay close attention when a recipe asks you to mix the dry and wet ingredients in separate bowls (you see this a lot in baking recipes). Mixing wet and dry ingredients separately helps make sure they combine and cook evenly. This is another good reason to read the recipe all the way through before starting to cook!

There are lots of ways to mix ingredients together, but some techniques are better for different types of recipes. Here are mixing words you'll see in recipes:

Stir

Stirring is the simplest mixing technique and is used in almost every recipe. It's when you use a spoon to mix ingredients until they're totally combined with each other.

Beat

Beating means to stir something quickly with a fork, spoon, whisk, or mixer until it becomes smooth. One ingredient you beat often is eggs, like in Confetti Birthday Cake (page 130).

Cream

Creaming entails beating ingredients together until a mixture becomes fluffy, usually sugar and softened butter. You'll cream ingredients often when making icing or cookies, like in Gingerbread People (page 150).

Whip

Whipping is beating something extremely quickly with a whisk or a mixer to make it light and airy. You most often whip heavy cream and sugar to make whipped cream, like in Splendid Sundaes (page 99).

Fold

Folding is the opposite of beating because you very slowly combine ingredients so they're not over-mixed. To fold ingredients, use a flexible spatula, scrape from the bottom of the bowl, and gently turn the mixture on top of itself. You fold in recipes like Kapow! Cupcakes (page 49).

KNIFE SKILLS

Another super important chef skill is learning how to cut things—what chefs call "knife skills." Knives and other sharp tools like blenders can be dangerous, so you should always (*always!*) ask a grown-up before you start a recipe that uses one of these tools.

How to Use a Knife

Before you pick up a knife, make sure your elbows are the same height as the kitchen counter; you might need a step stool. Place a wet kitchen towel underneath a cutting board to keep it from sliding. Find a knife that's sharp and feels comfortable. Since your hands are smaller than adult hands, it's best to use a chef's knife with a five- or six-inch blade. If you haven't used a chef's knife before, ask an adult to help with your technique or practice with a butter knife first.

To hold a knife, place the handle in the hand you write with (the blade should point away from you). Rest your thumb on the flat side of the blade that's closest to you (or side of the handle if that feels more steady) and curl your pointer finger on the other side of the blade. Then wrap your other three fingers around the handle.

Grip the food with your other hand using a claw or bridge grip. A claw grip is good for cutting large food like beefsteak tomatoes, lemons, or cucumbers. Make a claw with your hand, and (*very important!*) tuck your thumb behind your pointer finger. Dig your fingernails down into the food to keep it in place. For small stuff like cherry tomatoes or grapes, use a bridge grip by pinching the food with your pointer and thumb. They'll make a "bridge" over the food. The knife goes under your finger bridge as you cut one item at a time.

Cut the food with the flattest part of the food resting on the cutting board. Put the tip of the knife on the cutting board and, with a rocking motion, bring the handle end down to the cutting board. For extra strength, take the hand that's not holding the knife and place it on top of the blade. Make sure no part of any finger is under the blade and press down.

TYPES OF CUTS

Recipes may ask you to cut ingredients in a variety of ways. Here are a few types of cuts you'll come across in this book:

A   **Dice:** To cut a food (like tomato or celery) into cubes that are all the same size. Recipes often tell you the size cube to make.

B   **Mince:** To cut a food (like garlic) into very small cubes that are all the same size.

C   **Slice:** To cut a food (like apple or cucumber) into thin, similarly sized pieces or sometimes sticks.

D   **Chop:** To roughly cut a food (like broccoli or onion) into bite-size pieces, usually bigger pieces than dicing.

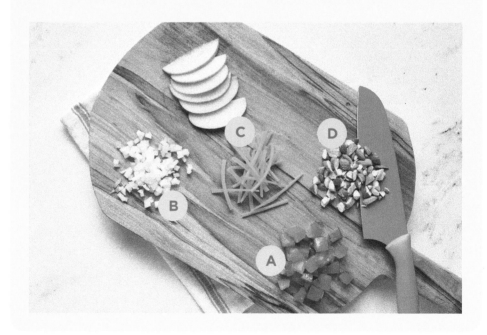

USING THE STOVE + OVEN

There are many types of stoves and every stove is slightly different, so ask your grown-up to explain to you exactly how yours works. And, of course, you should never (*never!*) use a stove without asking an adult first.

Stovetop Success

Before you cook on a stovetop, make sure the stovetop is around elbow height (you may need a step stool). Roll up any loose sleeves, tie back your hair if it's long, and stay focused: Watch the pan the whole time it is on the stove, don't leave the room, and set a timer to keep track of cook times. Other little tips to keep in mind include:

- Use utensils with long handles so your hands aren't too close to the heat.

- Turn the pan handles toward the center and back of the stove so you don't accidentally knock them off the stove.

- When you stir, hold the elbow of your stirring arm up high (to prevent burns) and hold the pan's handle in the other hand (to keep the pan from slipping). The handles of some pans are okay to touch without an oven mitt, but others get too hot. Ask your grown-up about the pans you have.

- When removing a pan from the stove, always use oven mitts. It's also a good idea to announce "Hot pan coming through!" so kitchen helpers can make way.

- Try to avoid grease splatters. Don't turn the heat up higher than the recipe suggests, and if you notice that your cooking oil is smoking, start over instead of adding ingredients to the oil. Use a new pan and start from the beginning.

- It is unlikely, but if a fire starts on the stovetop, quickly get a grown-up. Do not try to put it out.

Oven Care

Remember to adjust the height of the shelves in the oven before you turn it on, especially if you need to make room for more than one pan. And as with stovetop cooking, set a timer for the baking time so you don't burn your food. Better yet, set a timer for 5 to 10 minutes less than what the recipe says just in case your oven cooks faster. Other tips to keep in mind include:

- Use long oven mitts to protect you when taking things in and out. It can also be helpful to pull the oven shelf forward a little first, so you don't have to reach as far in.

- Stand away from the oven when you open it. Remember that the door to the oven is very, very hot, so make sure your legs are safe.

- Tell people you're opening the oven. It's a good idea to say "Opening the oven!" out loud so your kitchen helpers can step away.

- It is unlikely, but if a fire starts in the oven, keep the oven door closed. Do not try to put it out. Get a grown-up to turn off the oven.

PART TWO
The Parties

CHAPTER 3
Sleepovers

Nothing could be more fun than having your favorite friends for a sleepover. You can watch movies, play games, make crafts, and cook some delicious treats. And don't forget the best part . . . staying up late!

Since you'll be hanging out all night long and into the morning, you'll get a chance to serve your guests dinner and breakfast. You can prepare the Late Night Taco Bar (page 34) and Sleep Well Agua Fresca (page 32) recipes before everyone arrives. When it's time for dinner, your friends can have fun customizing their tacos with their favorite fillings and enjoying a tasty watermelon drink. In the morning, you can drag your tired selves into the kitchen to make pancakes together. These Berrylicious Oven Pancakes (page 38) are super cool because your friends can each decorate their own section with a fancy fruit design. In case anyone has a midnight snack attack, you might also want to set out some cheese and crackers.

SLEEP WELL AGUA FRESCA

SERVES 6 PREP TIME: 15 MINUTES CHILL TIME: 15 MINUTES

DAIRY-FREE, GLUTEN-FREE, NUT-FREE,
VEGETARIAN, VEGAN

TOOLS TO GATHER

Blender
Dry measuring cups and spoons
Liquid measuring cup
Chef's knife
Cutting board
Fine-mesh strainer
Serving pitcher or mixing bowl
  and ladle
Wooden spoon
Citrus reamer or press (optional)

INGREDIENTS TO HAVE

4 cups **pre-cut watermelon cubes**
1 **lime**
3 cups **water**, divided
1 teaspoon **granulated sugar**
24 **ice cubes** (for serving)

This watermelon drink is refreshing and perfect to tone down any taco heat! *Agua Fresca* means "fresh water" in Spanish, so it's best if you make it close to party time to keep the flavors fresh. You can also make this drink with other types of fruit (see note page 33).

1. **Combine watermelon and lime.** Place the watermelon cubes in a blender. ✋ Cut the lime in half and squeeze the juice from one half into the blender.

2. **Add sugar and water.** Measure 1½ cups water, add to the blender. Depending on how sweet your watermelon is, add sugar.

3. **Blend.** Blend until all the ingredients are combined.

4. **Strain the watermelon.** Set a mesh strainer over a medium-size bowl or a serving pitcher. Pour the watermelon juice into the strainer and use a wooden spoon to help push the liquid through. Discard the remaining watermelon pieces.

5. **Add more water and refrigerate.** Add the remaining 1½ cups water to the bowl or pitcher, stir with wooden spoon to combine. Refrigerate for at least 15 minutes, up to several hours.

6. **Serve.** Take out of the refrigerator and serve. Add lime wheels to the pitcher or bowl for a garnish (decoration). Serve with a bucket full of ice.

Swap it: If your grocery store doesn't have watermelon cubes, you'll need half of a baby watermelon and an adult who can cut it into cubes for you. Watermelon not your thing? Try strawberry, cantaloupe, pineapple, or honeydew melon. To make it extra special, add fresh herbs like mint to the blender!

LATE NIGHT TACO BAR

SERVES 4 TO 6 PREP TIME: 10 MINUTES COOK TIME: 20 MINUTES

DAIRY-FREE, GLUTEN-FREE, NUT-FREE

TOOLS TO GATHER

Large skillet
Wooden spoon
Chef's knife
Cutting board
Measuring spoons
Microwave-safe bowls
Colander

INGREDIENTS TO HAVE

2 tablespoons **olive oil**, divided
1 pound **ground turkey**
2 tablespoons **taco
   seasoning**, divided
3 **bell peppers**
2 medium **yellow onions**
12 (6-inch) **tortillas** of choice
1 (10-ounce) package **frozen corn**
1 (15.5-ounce) can **black beans**
   (low sodium or no-salt-added)

Get the energy you need to make it an all-nighter with these tasty tacos. Prepare all the taco fillings before your friends arrive and set them out buffet-style when it's time to eat. Serve it alongside toppings like your favorite salsa, Greek yogurt, shredded cheese, and hot sauce.

1. **Preheat the oven and pan.** Preheat the oven to 350°F. Put a large skillet over medium-high heat. Add 1 tablespoon olive oil to the frying pan and swirl to coat.

2. **Cook the turkey.** Add turkey to the frying pan. Wash hands and disinfect work surface. Add 1 tablespoon taco seasoning. Stir to coat and stir occasionally until the turkey is no longer pink (about 5 minutes). Remove from the heat, pour the turkey into a small bowl, and cover with aluminum foil.

3. **Cook the bell peppers and onions.** Slice bell peppers and onions into long strips. See How to Cut Bell Peppers and Onions (page 36). Turn the burner back to medium-high heat and add 1 tablespoon olive oil. Pour the sliced peppers and onions into the pan, then season with 1 tablespoon taco seasoning. Stir occasionally for 7 to 8 minutes until peppers and onions are soft. Pour into medium bowl and cover with foil.

4. **Prepare toppings.** 🖐 Wrap tortillas in aluminum foil, place in the oven for 15 minutes to warm. Microwave the corn in a small microwave-safe bowl according to package instructions, use oven mitts to take out. Drain the black beans in a colander and rinse bean-liquid away. Microwave the beans in a small microwave-safe bowl for 2 minutes, use oven mitts to take out.

5. **Serve.** Set up your taco bar buffet-style. In addition to the turkey, peppers and onions, corn, black beans, and tortillas, don't forget optional toppings like salsa, Greek yogurt, shredded cheese, and hot sauce.

Make ahead: You can cook the ground turkey, peppers, and onions ahead of time to speed up party prep. Store in airtight containers in the fridge for up to 3 days and microwave for a few minutes just before serving.

How to Cut Bell Peppers and Onions

Bell peppers and onions look like they're pretty tricky to cut, but if you follow these steps, they will be easy-peasy!

CUTTING BELL PEPPERS

First, use the tip of a chef's knife to cut a square shape around the stem.

Use your fingers to pull out the stem and as many seeds as you can. The bell pepper will now seem like a bowl. Carefully cut it in half, then put those pieces flat on the cutting board.

Cut those pieces in half, so you have four big pieces. With your fingers, remove the soft veins from the inside of the peppers and any remaining seeds. Now you're ready to cut the pepper into the shape the recipe calls for.

CUTTING ONIONS

HOW TO PEEL AN ONION

To peel an onion, cut off the end where the skin looks like crumpled paper. Peel the skin back to the other side, but don't tear off. The skin becomes a great handle for your non-cutting hand!

CUTTING ONION STRIPS OR DICING

Place the onion on the cutting board so the flat cut side is on the cutting board and the onion skin handle is facing up. Hold the onion skin handle with your non-cutting hand.

With a chef's knife, cut ½-inch vertical slices from the top (onion skin handle) down to the cutting board. Continue all the way through the onion.

If the recipe calls for onion strips, after you cut vertical slices, turn the onion on its side. Slice one time near the onion skin handle and voilà, you have strips. If the recipe calls for diced onion, you'll need to make a bunch of cuts after you turn it on its side. Slice ½-inch cuts, from the cut end toward the handle end.

CUTTING ONION RINGS

If a recipe calls for onion rings (great for topping In-Tents-ly Delicious Hamburgers, page 117), peel the same way. Place the onion on its side and hold the skin handle with your non-cutting hand. Slice from cut end to skin end, ½-inch at a time. Separate onion rings with your fingers.

HOW TO KEEP ONIONS FROM HURTING YOUR EYES

The best way to keep your eyes from tearing up when cutting onions is to use a very sharp knife. If it really bothers you, throw on a pair of swim goggles before you start cutting. (Just make sure you can see clearly!)

When you're finished cutting onions, wash your hands, cutting board, and knife right away so that it stops irritating your eyes.

BERRYLICIOUS OVEN PANCAKES

SERVES 4 TO 6 PREP TIME: 20 MINUTES COOK TIME: 15 MINUTES

NUT-FREE, VEGETARIAN

TOOLS TO GATHER:

Rimmed baking sheet

Mixing bowls

Flexible spatula

Measuring spoons

Dry measuring cups

Liquid measuring cup

Whisk

Colander

Chef's knife or butter knife

Cutting board

Parchment paper or nonstick spray

INGREDIENTS TO HAVE

2 cups **whole-wheat flour**

2 cups **all-purpose flour**

1 tablespoon **baking powder**

1 teaspoon **baking soda**

1 teaspoon **ground cinnamon**

½ teaspoon **salt**

4 **eggs**

2½ cups **milk** of choice

3 cups **fresh mixed berries**
(like strawberries,
blueberries, raspberries)

Let your friends join the cooking fun with this fun morning recipe. Take turns with the recipe steps or split into two teams and have one team make the batter while the other does berry prep and decor duty. Serve with maple syrup, confectioner's sugar, or whipped cream.

1. **Preheat the oven and prepare the pan.** ✋
Preheat the oven to 425°F. Line the rimmed baking sheet with parchment paper or spray with nonstick spray.

2. **Combine the dry ingredients.** In a large mixing bowl, combine the whole-wheat flour, all-purpose flour, baking powder, baking soda, ground cinnamon, and salt. Whisk to combine.

3. **Combine the wet ingredients.** In a medium mixing bowl, crack the eggs. Wash your hands and disinfect the work surface. Add milk to the bowl with the eggs. Whisk to combine.

4. **Finish the batter.** Pour the wet ingredients into the dry ingredient bowl. With a whisk, mix until completely combined and smooth. Pour the batter into the prepared baking sheet. Use the flexible spatula to spread the batter evenly across the whole pan.

5. **Decorate with berries.** Wash the berries. ✋ If using strawberries, slice the green tops off, then slice into pieces about ¼ inch thick. Place the berries in a pattern or design on the top of the batter.

6. **Bake.** 🤚 Bake in the oven for 15 minutes, or until golden brown.

7. **Serve.** Let cool for 5 minutes, then cut into 8 even rectangles with a butter knife. Serve 1 to 2 rectangles to each guest. Top with optional toppings like maple syrup, confectioner's sugar, or whipped cream.

Quick tip: Even if the recipe doesn't call for it, always crack eggs into a separate empty bowl just in case the shell breaks. That way, you don't have to worry about ruining the rest of your food. To rescue any shell bits that do make it into the bowl, use a big shell piece to scoop it out. This works much better than your fingers!

Build a Blanket Fort

Decorate your sleeping quarters by making a blanket fort for your friends! Ask your grown-up for help gathering supplies you can use for the fort: blankets or sheets, pillows, and chairs. Decide where to put your fort so it won't be in the way during the party. Then drape the blankets over the chairs and tie them to the chairs or secure with clothespins. You may need to use heavy chairs or put something heavy on the chairs, so they don't tip over. Fill the inside of the fort with pillows, blankets, games, stuffed animals, flashlights, and anything else your friends would like!

DIY Friendship Bracelets

Friendship bracelets are a cool sleepover activity because they double as a party favor. To make the bracelets, you need embroidery floss in different colors, craft scissors, and non-permanent tape like masking tape or painter's tape. If you've never made friendship bracelets before, ask a grown-up for help looking up patterns on the internet and print them out for your friends ahead of time. To begin, pick two to four colors of string, then cut each color long enough so it reaches from your shoulder to fingertips. Fold your strings in half and tie them together with a knot in the middle, leaving a loop above the knot. Tape the knot to the table to keep the bracelet in place while you work, then make your chosen design! You are finished when the bracelet is long enough to go around your wrist. Have a friend help you tie the bracelet on and cut off any extra string.

CHAPTER 4
Superhero Party

It's a bird, it's a plane, it's a . . . superhero party! Because superheroes need food to fuel their adventures, this party features a Super Snack Buffet and a Super Snack-tivity. Invite your guests to come dressed as their favorite superhero or action star so they can help you save the day.

For your Super Snack Buffet, make the Super Smoothie drink (page 44) and the Kapow! Cupcakes (page 49) in advance. Round out your buffet with snacks like pretzels, hummus, and grapes. When your guests arrive, combine powers to make Superhero Shield Tortillas (page 46), and customize them with your own superhero symbol before fueling up.

SUPER SMOOTHIE

SERVES 4 PREP TIME: 5 MINUTES

DAIRY-FREE, GLUTEN-FREE, NUT-FREE, VEGETARIAN

TOOLS TO GATHER

Blender
Dry measuring cups
Liquid measuring cup

INGREDIENTS TO HAVE

1 **ripe banana**
¾ cup **frozen pineapple**
¾ cup **frozen blueberries**
1½ cups **plain soymilk** (or milk of choice)

Power up with this smoothie and you'll be leaping over buildings and catching the bad guys! Pineapple and blueberries combine to make the potent purple color that will wow the superhero gang. Plus, it blends faster than a speeding bullet, leaving you plenty of time to save the day (or hang out with your friends).

1. **Banana.** Peel 1 ripe banana, then put it in the blender. ✋
2. **Add the pineapple and blueberries.** Pour the frozen pineapple and frozen blueberries into the blender.
3. **Add the milk.** Pour the milk into the blender.
4. **Blend.** Blend the smoothie until all ingredients are combined.
5. **Serve.** Pour into 4 glasses or into a pitcher for guests to serve themselves.

> **Make ahead:** For the brightest purple possible, serve the smoothie right away. You can make it a few hours ahead and store in the fridge, but make sure to keep it in a tightly sealed container to keep it purple-y. Place the smoothie in a lidded pitcher on the buffet just before guests arrive and set out clear cups.

Decorate Your Superhero Buffet

Decorate the wall behind the buffet graffiti-style, with some superhero-inspired word cutouts. Start with sheets of construction paper in different colors and cut them into burst shapes. With a black marker, write a different comic action on each burst, like "Pow!" "Wham!" "Bam!" "Bang!" Be sure to make the letters thick so your guests can read them from far away. When you're finished, tape them to windows with clear tape or to walls and doors with non-permanent tape like masking tape or painter's tape.

Take it to the next level by creating paper labels for fruits and veggies to let your guests know what superpowers they'll gain by eating them. Cut out small bursts and write superpowers on them (ideas: "Invisibility," "Energy Boost," "X-Ray Vision"). Tape the small bursts to toothpicks. Serve each fruit and veggie in an individual bowl and place a superpower label in each.

SUPERHERO SHIELD TORTILLAS

SERVES 4 PREP TIME: 20 MINUTES COOK TIME: 10 MINUTES

NUT-FREE, VEGETARIAN

TOOLS TO GATHER

Blender or food processor
Chef's knife
Cutting board
Measuring spoons
Dry measuring cups
Mixing bowl
Fine-mesh strainer
Wooden spoon
2 baking sheets
3-inch cookie cutters (or a
    butter knife)
Wide spatula

INGREDIENTS TO HAVE

4 (8-inch) **tortillas** of choice
3 **ripe tomatoes**
2 **limes**, divided
¼ teaspoon **ground cumin**
¼ teaspoon **garlic powder**
¼ teaspoon **salt**
4 slices **sliced cheese** (cheddar,
    pepper Jack, or Monterey Jack)
½ cup **shredded cheese**
1 (18-ounce) container
    plain Greek yogurt

Ward off evil—and hunger—with these delicious shields! Superhero Shield Tortillas are a version of a tostada, a Mexican dish that resembles a flat crunchy taco. Every hero should design their own shield, so make these with your friends at the party.

1. **Preheat the oven and prepare the pans.** Set the oven racks with room for 2 pans and preheat the oven to 375°F. Place 2 tortillas on each baking sheet, then set aside.

2. **Pulse the tomatoes.** Quarter the tomatoes (see How to Cut Tomatoes, page 48). Put the tomatoes in a blender or food processor and pulse for about 10 short bursts. Don't over-pulse or you'll have a tomato smoothie.

3. **Strain the tomatoes.** Set a mesh strainer over a medium mixing bowl. Pour the tomatoes into the strainer (watch out for the blade!). Use a wooden spoon to press liquid out of the tomatoes. Discard the liquid and pour tomatoes into a mixing bowl.

4. **Season the salsa.** Cut the first lime in half and add juice from one of the halves to the mixing bowl, saving the second half for later. Add ground cumin, garlic powder, and salt to the mixing bowl. Stir to combine.

5. **Add your superhero crest.** Put the 4 cheese slices on a clean cutting board. Cut them into your individual superhero symbols (like a star or your initials) with a cookie cutter or by cutting your own design with a butter knife. Place 1 cheese symbol in the middle of each tortilla.

6. **Add salsa and shredded cheese.** Add 2 tablespoons shredded cheese to the edge of each tortilla, using your fingers to pinch it into a stripe about ½-inch wide. Add 2 tablespoons salsa to each tortilla (making a stripe between your superhero symbol and the shredded cheese).

7. **Bake.** ✋ Put both trays in the oven and bake for 8 to 10 minutes. Use the oven light to watch the tortillas closely; bake them long enough that the cheese bubbles, but not so long that you can't tell what your superhero crest is anymore.

8. **Serve.** To make a crema sauce, cut the second lime. Squeeze 3 lime halves into the Greek yogurt container and stir to combine. While still warm, serve each guest one tortilla with crema and extra salsa on the side.

Quick tip: To make your superhero symbol look extra awesome, keep your cheese slices cold in the fridge until just before you cut them. Once you cut your shape with a cookie cutter or knife, peel the extra cheese away from the shape. When you put the salsa on the shield, make sure it isn't touching the symbol in the middle.

How to Cut Tomatoes

Tomatoes are another vegetable that can be confusing to cut, but with a little practice they'll be no problem! If you have a serrated knife (the kind with the bumpy blade), it can make cutting tomatoes easier, but a regular chef's knife works too.

HOW TO CUT LARGE TOMATOES (BEEFSTEAK OR ROMA)

Remember to hold the tomato with the claw grip and to use the correct grip on the knife (see Knife Skills, page 24). Slice off the stem and use the tip of the knife to cut a circle around the hard part where the stem used to be (the core). Pull out the core with your fingers. Place the tomato cut-side down, which will keep it from rolling.

TO QUARTER THE TOMATO

Cut the tomato in half, then put the halves flat-side down. Cut these halves in half again to make four pieces total.

TO SLICE THE TOMATO

With the cut side facedown, make up and down cuts from right to left (if you're right-handed) or left to right (if you're left-handed).

TO DICE THE TOMATO

Slice the tomato first (see above), then put all the slices flat on the cutting board. Cut each slice into strips. Rotate the cutting board and cut all the strips in the other direction to make cubes.

HOW TO CUT SMALL TOMATOES (CHERRY OR GRAPE)

Hold the tomato using the bridge grip, pinching between your pointer finger and thumb. Cut between your two fingers (see Knife Skills, page 24).

KAPOW! CUPCAKES

MAKES 12 CUPCAKES PREP TIME: 15 MINUTES COOK TIME: 20 MINUTES

NUT-FREE, VEGETARIAN

TOOLS TO GATHER

Food processor or blender
Muffin tin
12 cupcake liners
Mixing bowls
Dry measuring cups and spoons
Liquid measuring cup
Whisk
Flexible spatula
Spoon

INGREDIENTS TO HAVE

⅓ cup **oil** (canola, avocado, or
 sunflower oil)
½ cup plus 2 tablespoons **milk** of
 choice, divided
1 **ripe banana**
1 (5-ounce) package **baby spinach**
1½ teaspoons **vanilla
 extract**, divided
1 **egg**
2 cups **all-purpose flour**
⅔ cup **granulated sugar**
2 teaspoons **baking powder**
½ teaspoon **baking soda**
¼ teaspoon **salt**
1 cup **confectioner's sugar**

These cupcakes will give you super strength because of their hidden superpower ingredient: spinach! Don't worry, though; only someone with superhuman tasting powers can taste the spinach, and it can be your secret because the cupcakes mostly taste like banana. A quick glaze-style icing adds the Kapow! burst to the cupcakes.

1. **Preheat the oven and prepare the pan.** Preheat the oven to 350°F. Line a muffin pan with 12 cupcake liners.

2. **Process the wet ingredients.** Add the following to a food processor (or blender if you don't have a food processor): oil, ½ cup milk, banana, baby spinach, 1 teaspoon vanilla extract, and egg. Process until all ingredients are completely combined.

3. **Mix the dry ingredients.** In a large mixing bowl, pour in the all-purpose flour, sugar, baking powder, baking soda, and salt. Whisk until combined.

4. **Combine the wet and dry ingredients.** Pour the spinach puree into the dry-ingredient bowl. Be careful you don't pour out the blade! Fold together with a rubber spatula by gently scraping from the bottom of the bowl and turning the mixture on top of itself until just combined.

CONTINUED

5. **Bake.** Scoop the batter into the prepared tray, using a quarter cup measuring cup to fill each cupcake slot about two-thirds of the way. 👋 Bake for 18 to 22 minutes, until cupcake is firm to touch.

6. **Make the icing.** In a small mixing bowl, combine confectioner's sugar, ½ teaspoon vanilla extract, and 2 tablespoons milk.

7. **Decorate.** Wait until the cupcakes are completely cool to decorate. If icing hardens before you're ready to decorate, just stir to soften. To make a Kapow! burst shape: Use a spoon to drizzle icing in the shape's outline, then drag the icing with the spoon to fill in the center. Icing will harden after a few minutes.

Make ahead: You can bake the cupcakes up to 2 days before the party. Let the cupcakes cool completely, then store the cupcakes only (with no icing) in a food storage container at room temperature. Do not refrigerate; it dries out the cupcakes! Then make the icing and decorate the cupcakes right before your party.

Superhero Mask Craft

Spend the party transformed with these masks! To set up, you'll need a paper plate for each guest and a few sheets of thick paper like construction paper or card stock. You'll also need materials to decorate the masks (like markers, pipe cleaners, sequins, paint, glitter, or colored paper). Finally, gather up scissors, glue, and tape or a stapler.

Cut the paper plate in half and cut one half into the shape of the mask you want to make. Cut eye holes by using the scissors to punch two small holes, then use the scissors to cut them larger. (Note: don't punch the eye holes while the mask is on your face!) Try it on to make sure you can see. Decorate your mask to match your superhero identity. To keep the mask on your face, cut two long strips of thick paper and attach one to each side of the mask with tape or a stapler. Put the mask on and get a friend to help you adjust the two paper strips tight enough, then secure with tape or a staple. Now fly up, up, and away!

CHAPTER 5
Movie Marathon

Walk the red carpet when you turn your living room into a movie theater for a Movie Marathon party! Pick a theme for your marathon (like cartoons, sci-fi, sports, fairy tales), gather your moviegoers, and serve them food from your DIY snack stand as they watch.

Make the Hollywood Walk of Fame Cookies (page 59) and the syrup for the Mango Movie Star Sparkler drink (page 54) up to two days in advance. Before the guests arrive, pop the popcorn and set up a Perfect Movie Popcorn bar (page 56). Just before the first movie starts, encourage your guests to fill their popcorn bag, and assemble and serve the Sparkler drink. When the credits are about to start rolling, serve the cookies.

MANGO MOVIE STAR SPARKLER

SERVES 6 PREP TIME: 10 MINUTES CHILL TIME: 30 MINUTES

DAIRY-FREE, GLUTEN-FREE, NUT-FREE,
VEGETARIAN

TOOLS TO GATHER

Large stockpot
Dry measuring cups
Liquid measuring cup
Blender
Fine-mesh strainer
Mixing bowl
Wooden spoon

INGREDIENTS TO HAVE

4 cups **frozen mango cubes**
2 **limes**
⅓ cup **granulated sugar**
1 cup **water**
1 liter **unflavored soda water**
24 ice cubes (for serving)

Sipping this sunny yellow sparkler will make your guests feel like movie stars. This fizzy mango-lime drink will transport them to a pool with a view of palm trees and the Hollywood sign off in the distance. Make the syrup in advance to save precious movie time.

1. **Mix the mango syrup.** Put the mango in the large stockpot. ✋ Cut 1 lime in half, squeeze juice from both halves into the pot. Add the sugar and water to the pot. Stir to combine.

2. **Cook the mango syrup.** ✋ Put the pot over medium high heat. Bring the mango syrup to a low boil, or just when you start to hear bubbles making noise (about 3 minutes). Remove from the heat.

3. **Blend the mango syrup.** ✋ Carefully (the pot is still hot!) pour mango and hot liquid into a blender, then blend until smooth.

4. **Strain and chill mango syrup.** Set a fine-mesh strainer over the medium mixing bowl. Pour the blended mango into the strainer, then use a wooden spoon to help press all the liquid through the strainer. Discard (or eat!) the mango pieces. Let the syrup chill in the fridge for at least 30 minutes, or up to 2 days, in an airtight container.

5. **Serve.** Set out 6 glasses and add 4 ice cubes to each glass. Using a liquid measuring cup, pour ½ cup mango syrup into each glass, then top off each glass with ½ cup soda water. ✋ Garnish with a lime wedge (see tip below) and serve right away.

Decorate: Give the cups that movie-star sparkle by garnishing each glass with a lime wedge. Wash lime and cut in half. Put the 2 halves on the cutting board with the cut side down. Hold with the claw grip (see Knife Skills, page 24) and cut down toward the center of the lime, slicing each half into 3 triangle-shaped wedges. Make a cut to the center of each wedge so it will sit on the rim of the glass. Now enjoy each glamorous sip!

Spotlight on the Popcorn Bar

Make signs with paper and markers to explain your popcorn bar. Make a big one that says: "Welcome to [Your Name]'s Movie Theater. 1) Scoop two cups popcorn into the bag. 2) Add one to two spoonfuls of toppings. 3) Hold the bag closed and shake."
  Tape that sign to the table near the popcorn bowl. Fold three small pieces of paper in half to make little tent shapes that will stand up on their own. Write "Spicy Taco Topping: cumin + cayenne + squeeze of lime," "Cinnamon Sugar Topping," and "Italian-Style Topping: Parmesan + thyme" on the tents and set them in front of the toppings bowls so people know what they're eating!

PERFECT MOVIE POPCORN

SERVES **4 TO 6** PREP TIME: **15 MINUTES** COOK TIME: **5 MINUTES**

GLUTEN-FREE, NUT-FREE, VEGETARIAN

TOOLS TO GATHER

8 paper lunch bags
Dry measuring cups and spoons
Microwave-safe plate and bowl
Mixing bowls
Spoons
Cutting board
Chef's knife
Craft scissors

INGREDIENTS TO HAVE

½ cup **popcorn kernels**, divided
1 teaspoon **oil** (canola, avocado, or
   sunflower), divided
¼ cup **unsalted butter**
½ teaspoon **salt**, divided
4 teaspoons **ground cumin**
⅛ teaspoon **cayenne** (optional)
1 **lime**
2 tablespoons **granulated sugar**
½ teaspoon **ground cinnamon**
½ cup shredded or
   grated **parmesan**
Small bunch **fresh thyme**

Sure, you *can* watch a movie without popcorn, but why would you want to? Impress your guests with the option to sprinkle on three different fancy toppings as they settle in to watch the show. Make the popcorn and toppings before they arrive and set them out buffet-style so guests can customize their own movie-watching treat.

1. **Pop 2 bags popcorn.** Measure ¼ cup popcorn kernels and pour into a paper bag. Measure ½ teaspoon oil and pour into the same bag. Fold the top over 3 times (don't seal with tape, staples, or anything else). Shake the bag to coat kernels with oil. Place the bag on its side on a microwave-safe plate, and microwave. You'll know the popcorn is done when the popping noises begin to slow down (2 to 4 minutes). Use oven mitts to take out of the microwave. Repeat for the second bag.

2. **Butter the popcorn.** Put butter in a small microwave-safe bowl. Microwave in 10 second bursts until butter is completely melted. Use oven mitts to take out of the microwave. Carefully open the popcorn bags (hot steam will come out). Pour about half of the butter into each bag. Pour ¼ teaspoon salt into each bag. Refold the tops of the bags and shake to coat.

3. **Make the Spicy Taco topping.** Add ground cumin to a small bowl. If you want to make it spicy, add between a pinch and ⅛ teaspoon cayenne to the cumin and stir. Cut a lime into wedges and place on a plate.

4. **Make the Cinnamon Sugar topping.** Add the sugar and cinnamon to a small bowl. Stir to combine.

5. **Make the Italian-Style topping.** Pour the parmesan into a small bowl. Pick off the leaves of about 10 sprigs of thyme until you have 2 teaspoons thyme leaves. Add the thyme to the parmesan and stir to combine.

6. **Serve.** Cut 6 clean lunch bags with scissors so they're 5 inches tall. Set up a popcorn bag assembly buffet with the popcorn bowl and a 1-cup scoop, each of the 3 toppings bowls with a teaspoon, and the lime wedges near the Spicy Taco topping.

DIY Popcorn Bags

Your guests can make their own popcorn bags for the Perfect Movie Popcorn. Collect paper lunch bags (white or brown) for each guest, markers or crayons, stickers, and scissors. Cut the bag so it's about five inches tall. Have guests create designs; they can draw popcorn, make red stripes like in the movie theater, write their names, draw movie characters, or anything they'd like! Then the bags are ready to hold their popcorn in style while they watch the movie.

How to Measure Butter

Did you know that you can measure butter without measuring spoons or cups? There are measuring marks right on the butter wrapper that make it so much easier! Look at a stick of butter still in its wrapper, and notice the lines that say "1 TBSP." Each one of those lines is the amount of butter you need to cut to get one tablespoon. Take a chef's knife and line up the blade with the measurement line for the amount you need. Then, use your knife to cut the butter, label and all. Remove the wrapper and add the butter to the recipe. Easy-peasy!

  Sometimes recipes list the amount of butter in cups instead of tablespoons. If you ever see that, here's a handy list of equivalent measurements so you know how to measure:

⅛ cup butter = 2 tablespoons = ¼ stick of butter

¼ cup butter = 4 tablespoons = ½ stick of butter

½ cup butter = 8 tablespoons = 1 whole stick of butter

¾ cup butter = 12 tablespoons = 1½ sticks of butter

1 cup butter = 16 tablespoons = 2 whole sticks of butter

HOLLYWOOD WALK OF FAME COOKIES

**MAKES 12 COOKIES PREP TIME: 15 MINUTES
CHILL TIME: 1 HOUR BAKE TIME: 8 TO 10 MINUTES**

NUT-FREE, VEGETARIAN

TOOLS TO GATHER

Baking sheet
Parchment paper or silicone
   baking mat
Dry measuring cups and spoons
Mixing bowls
Microwave-safe bowl
Whisk
Plastic wrap
Rolling pin
Flexible spatula
Star cookie cutter or butter knife
Cooling rack (optional)

INGREDIENTS TO HAVE

3 tablespoons **unsalted butter**
1 cup **all-purpose flour**
¾ teaspoon **cornstarch**
¼ teaspoon **baking powder**
½ cup **granulated sugar**
¼ teaspoon **salt**
1 teaspoon **ground cinnamon**
1½ teaspoons **vanilla extract**
1 **egg**
**Gold sanding sugar, gel
   icing, food coloring pen** for
   decorating (optional)

Walk the walk with these Walk of Fame–inspired cinnamon sugar cookies! With optional decorating tools like a food coloring pen, gel icing, and gold sanding sugar, your guests can enjoy the magic of a little sprinkle of stardust.

1. **Preheat the oven, prepare the pan, melt the butter.** Preheat the oven to 350°F. Line the baking sheet with parchment paper or a silicone baking mat. Melt the butter in the microwave for 10 seconds at a time until completely melted.

2. **Mix the dry ingredients.** In a medium mixing bowl, add the all-purpose flour, cornstarch, baking powder, sugar, salt, and cinnamon. Whisk to combine.

3. **Mix the wet ingredients.** In a large mixing bowl, add the melted butter, vanilla extract, and egg. Beat with the whisk to combine.

4. **Fold the wet and dry ingredients together.** Add a little bit of the dry ingredients into the wet ingredient bowl, use the flexible spatula to fold together. Continue adding dry ingredients a little bit at a time, until all the ingredients have been totally combined.

CONTINUED

5. **Shape the dough and chill.** Cut a 2-foot long piece of plastic wrap and put on the counter. Place the dough in the middle of the plastic wrap, and shape until it's a rectangle 1 inch thick. Cut another 2-foot-long piece of plastic wrap and place on top of the dough. Chill dough in fridge for 1 hour or up to 3 days.

6. **Roll out the dough and cut stars.** With a rolling pin, roll the dough between the layers of plastic wrap until it's a long rectangle about ⅛ inch thick. Press the star cookie cutter into the dough or use a butter knife to trace star shapes. Peel away the dough scraps and form a new ball of dough. Place the stars on the baking sheet. Repeat with the extra dough in the scrap ball, making about 12 cookies total.

7. **Bake.** 🖐 Bake cookies for 8 to 10 minutes. They will get harder as they cool. Let cool for 5 minutes, then transfer to the wire rack to cool completely. Use gold sanding sugar or decorate as you like!

Decorate: Make your stars look like the Hollywood Walk of Fame by decorating them! With a black food coloring marker, you can draw a movie camera and write your guests' names on the stars. Use black gel icing to trace around the edges and to draw a circle in the middle. Sprinkle gold sanding sugar on top of the icing to make the stars sparkly.

CHAPTER 6
Tea Party

It's high time for tea! Invite your guests to wear their fanciest dress-up jewelry, dresses, bow ties, suspenders, blazers, or hats to the party. When they arrive, they'll be treated to an elegant sit-down of tea sandwiches, cake, and of course, tea!

Bake the Mini Orange Cakes (page 69) and make the cream cheese spread for the Tiny Tea Sandwiches (page 67) up to a day in advance. Prepare the whipped cream for the cakes and assemble the sandwiches just before the party starts so the whipped cream is fresh, and the bread doesn't get soggy. Make the tea once your guests arrive and are ready to be seated. Serve the tea, sandwiches, and cake all together—perhaps alongside some optional jams and scones—and your afternoon tea will be fit for royalty.

I'M A LITTLE TEAPOT

SERVES **4** PREP TIME: **15 MINUTES**

DAIRY-FREE, GLUTEN-FREE, NUT-FREE, VEGETARIAN

TOOLS TO GATHER

Stovetop or electric tea kettle (or small stockpot)
Liquid measuring cup
Chef's knife
Cutting board
Serving teapot (optional)
4 teacups or mugs
Creamer bowl
Sugar bowl
Loose-leaf tea bag (optional)

INGREDIENTS TO HAVE

4 cups **water**
4 tea bags of **decaffeinated tea** (or 4 teaspoons loose-leaf tea)
Milk (optional)
Lemon (optional)
Sugar cubes (optional)
Honey (optional)

A tea party without tea is just . . . well . . . a party! And where's the fun in that? There are lots of types of decaffeinated tea to choose from. Some of my favorites are Earl Grey, English breakfast, jasmine green, rooibos, peppermint, and chamomile. Serve it in a fancy teapot alongside milk, lemon, sugar cubes, and honey.

1. **Preheat the teapot.** Fill the serving teapot with warm tap water so the tea will stay warmer longer.

2. **Boil the water.** Boil the water 🤚 using a stovetop tea kettle, electric tea kettle, or stock pot. For more instructions, see Teatime Tips (page 66).

3. **Pour the water into the teapot.** Pour out the warm tap water from the serving teapot. 🤚 Very carefully, pour the boiling water into the teapot. Keep your non-pouring hand out of the way (don't hold the teapot with it) so you don't burn yourself if you spill.

4. **Add tea.** If using tea bags, add the tea bags to the serving pot and shut the lid. If using loose-leaf tea, place tea in the loose-leaf tea bag, tie the top, and add to the teapot.

5. **Steep the tea.** Set a timer to steep your tea for the right amount. Follow the directions on the box of tea for steeping time.

6. **Meanwhile, prepare optional mix-ins.** Slice a lemon into wedges and place on a plate. Pour milk into a creamer bowl, place sugar cubes in a sugar dish, and set out honey.

7. **Serve.** Remove tea bags from the serving pot. Pour tea into 4 teacups or mugs (hold the teapot lid so it doesn't come off). Tell your guests to wait a few minutes for tea to cool before drinking.

Swap it: No teapot? No problem! Preheat 4 teacups or mugs by filling with warm tap water. When your boiling water is ready, dump the warm tap water out of the teacups, and very carefully pour boiling water into the mugs. Remember to keep your non-pouring hand out of the way (don't hold the mug!) so you don't burn yourself if you spill. Then, put one tea bag in each mug, and steep tea according to the tea box's instructions.

Sugar Cube Balance Game

This hilarious minute-to-win-it-style game will be sure to make all your fancy guests a little less proper. Gather extra sugar cubes (not the ones you'll serve with tea later) and a spoon for each guest. Have your first contestant hold the handle side of a spoon with his or her mouth. Tell the contestant to stack as many sugar cubes on the spoon as they can within one minute. Set a timer for 60 seconds and have the contestant begin. If the tower falls, the contestant can rebuild the tower as many times as needed within the minute. Count how many sugar cubes are in the tower when the timer goes off. Repeat with each guest. The tallest sugar cube tower wins bragging rights!

Teatime Tips

There are many types of tea, but three of the most common are black (like Earl Grey, English breakfast, or chai), herbal (like rooibos, chamomile, or peppermint), and green. Green tea needs the lowest temperature water and steeps for the shortest length of time. Herbal tea needs the hottest temperature water and steeps for the longest, and black tea is in the middle.

How to figure out the right way to brew with different boil methods? Check out the handy chart below, and double check the tea box for steeping time.

	GREEN TEA	BLACK TEA	HERBAL TEA
STOVETOP KETTLE	When steam just starts to come out of the spout (before it whistles), pour into the teapot. Steep 2 to 3 minutes.	When the kettle whistles, let cool with the lid off for 1 minute before pouring into the teapot. Steep 4 to 5 minutes.	When the kettle whistles, pour into the teapot right away. Steep 3 to 6 minutes.
ELECTRIC KETTLE	When the kettle turns off, open lid and wait 5 minutes to cool before pouring into the teapot. Steep 2 to 3 minutes.	When the kettle turns off, open lid and wait 1 minute to cool before pouring into the teapot. Steep 4 to 5 minutes.	When the kettle turns off, pour water into the teapot right away. Steep 3 to 6 minutes.
STOCKPOT	Over high heat, bring water to a low boil (about 4 minutes) before pouring into the teapot. You should see a bunch of small bubbles under the water's surface but not on top. Steep 2 to 3 minutes.	Over high heat, bring water to a full boil (about 5½ minutes) before pouring into the teapot. You should be just starting to see big bubbles on the surface of the water. Steep 4 to 5 minutes.	Over high heat, bring water to a full boil for about 30 seconds (about 6 minutes total) before pouring into teapot. Steep 3 to 6 minutes.

TINY TEA SANDWICHES

SERVES 6 PREP TIME: 30 MINUTES

NUT-FREE, VEGETARIAN

TOOLS TO GATHER

2 cutting boards

Chef's knife

Kitchen scissors or clean
   craft scissors

Dry measuring cups and spoons

Microwave-safe mixing bowl

Spoon

Butter knife

INGREDIENTS TO HAVE

2 (8-ounce) packages
   cream cheese

12 slices **soft sandwich bread**

1 **apple**

2 **lemons**

Small bunch **green onions**

Small bunch **fresh dill**

⅛ teaspoon **black pepper**

At afternoon tea service in England, people enjoy yummy tea sandwiches. They're made with soft bread and cut neatly into small shapes so you can eat them daintily with your tea. For different versions, substitute the apple with sliced cucumber, arrange smoked salmon on top of the cream cheese, or fill the sandwiches with egg salad.

1. **Prepare the cream cheese, bread, and apple.** Scoop cream cheese into medium microwave-safe mixing bowl and set aside. Using a chef's knife, cut crusts off the 12 slices of bread. Chop around the apple core to make 4 big pieces. Slice the apple pieces into ¼-inch-thick slices.

2. **Make the cream cheese spread.** Cut the lemons in half, then squeeze the juice from all 4 halves into the bowl with the cream cheese. With kitchen scissors or clean craft scissors, cut the green onions into ¼-inch pieces until you have ¼ cup. Pour into the bowl. Cut the dill into smaller pieces with scissors until you have ¼ cup dill. Pour into the bowl. Add black pepper. Microwave in 10-second bursts until the cream cheese is soft enough to stir (about 30 seconds). Stir the cream cheese spread until combined.

CONTINUED

3. **Assemble the sandwiches.** Using a butter knife, spread about 2 table-spoons cream cheese spread on 1 slice of bread. Place 4 to 5 apple slices on top. Spread about 2 tablespoons cream cheese on a second slice of bread, and place on top to make a sandwich. Repeat for the remaining 5 sandwiches.

4. **Cut the sandwiches into triangles.** Using a chef's knife, cut sandwiches in half on the diagonal (from corner to corner). Rotate sandwich, and cut on other diagonal, making 4 triangles total. Repeat for remaining 5 sandwiches.

5. **Serve.** Chill for at least 15 minutes, or until ready to serve. Serve each guest 4 triangles.

Decorate: Tea sandwiches are traditionally cut into triangles, but you can cut them into fun shapes with a cookie cutter instead! With a 3-inch-wide cookie cutter, cut your bread into shapes in step 1 (instead of cutting crusts off bread). Then, just spread the cream cheese spread and add apples like in steps 2 and 3, and skip cutting them into triangles in step 4.

Set the Table

Here are just a few ideas to set your table afternoon tea–style! Place a tablecloth or lace doilies on the table. Arrange fresh flowers in a vase in the middle of the table. Sprinkle some flower petals over the tablecloth. Set the table with fancy plates, teacups or mugs, and cloth napkins. Arrange the tea sandwiches in a pretty pattern on a tiered serving tray or platter. Or place the cakes on a cake stand.

MINI ORANGE CAKES

SERVES 4 PREP TIME: 20 MINUTES COOK TIME: 30 MINUTES

NUT-FREE, VEGETARIAN

TOOLS TO GATHER

4 ramekins and baking sheet (or
    muffin tin with liners)
Nonstick spray
Mixing bowls
Dry measuring cups and spoons
Liquid measuring cup
Whisk
Grater
Flexible spatula
Chef's knife
Cutting board
Electric mixer or stand mixer

INGREDIENTS TO HAVE

1 cup **all-purpose flour**
¾ teaspoon **baking powder**
⅛ teaspoon **salt**
½ cup plus 1 tablespoon
    granulated sugar, divided
⅓ cup **olive oil**
2 **eggs**
3 **navel oranges**
1 cup **heavy whipping cream**

These adorable tiny cakes look fancy enough to serve to a queen or king but are simple enough for non-royals to bake! Your afternoon tea should be a relaxing time for you and your friends, so you can make the cakes a day in advance (store in an airtight container at room temperature), then whip up the orange whipped cream just before serving.

1. **Preheat the oven, prepare the ramekins, chill the bowl and beaters.** Preheat the oven to 350°F. Set the ramekins on the baking sheet, coat each ramekin with nonstick spray. Chill the large mixing bowl and electric mixer beaters in the freezer.

2. **Mix the dry ingredients.** In a large mixing bowl, combine the all-purpose flour, baking powder, salt, and ½ cup of the sugar. Whisk thoroughly.

3. **Mix the wet ingredients.** Pour the olive oil into the medium mixing bowl. Crack the eggs into a small mixing bowl, fish out any shell bits, then pour into the olive oil bowl. Beat with the whisk until combined. Pour into the bowl with the dry ingredients, then beat to combine.

4. **Add the orange zest.** Zest 2 oranges with a grater. Measure 1 tablespoon of zest and add to mixing bowl, saving the rest for later.

CONTINUED

5. **Add the orange juice.** 🖐 Cut the 2 oranges in half. Squeeze the juice from the 2 oranges into a liquid measuring cup (see Juice Citrus Like a Pro, page 89). Keep squeezing until you have 1 cup orange juice. Pour ⅓ cup orange juice into a mixing bowl, then put remaining ⅔ cup in the fridge to chill. Beat the orange juice and zest into the batter with the whisk until combined.

6. **Bake the cakes and let cool.** Use the flexible spatula to divide the batter into 4 ramekins, filling each about ¾ full. 🖐 Bake for 30 to 35 minutes, or when a knife inserted into the center comes out clean. Let cool before decorating.

7. **Make the orange whipped cream.** Remove the bowl and beaters from the freezer. Add heavy whipping cream, 1 tablespoon sugar, and ⅔ cup orange juice to the cold bowl. Whip the cream for 2 to 10 minutes, until it forms stiff peaks (see How to Make Whipped Cream, page 100 for more whipped cream hints).

8. **Garnish and serve**. Once the cakes are completely cooled, add a few dollops of whipped cream to the top of each cake. For the garnish, slice the third orange in half, then thinly slice into semicircles. Place 1 orange slice on top of each cake. Sprinkle remaining orange zest on top.

Swap it: Don't have ramekins? Make cupcakes instead! Line a muffin tin with 8 cupcake liners. Fill the liners about ⅔ of the way up, making 8 cupcakes. Bake for 18 to 22 minutes, or when a clean knife inserted into the center comes out clean.

CHAPTER 7
Pizza Party

Who can pass up a pizza party? And this one boasts not one but two pizza delights! Make your dinner pizza together and then, continue the theme with a surprise dessert pizza for your second course. Wash it all down with a yummy homemade grape soda.

Prepare the Rainbow Fruit Pizza (page 81) and the syrup for the Great Grape Soda (page 74) a few hours before your guests arrive. Make the A Pizza My Heart (page 76) as a group during the party. Assemble the soda while the pizza's baking and serve it along with the pizza. You could ask one of your guests to bring a green salad—or something extra healthy—but the fruit pizza recipe will do the trick, too. Just serve it with forks for dessert.

GREAT GRAPE SODA

SERVES 6 PREP TIME: 20 MINUTES CHILL TIME: 30 MINUTES

DAIRY-FREE, GLUTEN-FREE, NUT-FREE, VEGETARIAN

TOOLS TO GATHER

Large stockpot
Dry measuring cups
Liquid measuring cup
Potato masher or fork
Blender
Fine-mesh strainer
Mixing bowl
Wooden spoon
Paper straws (optional)

INGREDIENTS TO HAVE

2 pounds **seedless grapes**
2 **lemons**
⅓ cup **granulated sugar**
1 liter **unflavored soda water**
24 **ice cubes** (for serving)

Nothing goes better with hot pizza than cold soda! This soda is made with fresh grapes and tastes just like fizzy grape juice. The color will change depending on whether you use red, green, or purple grapes, but all taste and look perfectly grapealicious!

1. **Mix the grape syrup.** Pick grapes off stems and wash. Measure 4 cups of grapes and place in the large stockpot. Cut 1 lemon in half, squeeze juice from both halves into the pot. Add the sugar and 1 cup water to the pot. Stir to combine.

2. **Cook the grape syrup.** Put the pot over medium high heat. Bring grapes to a low boil, or just when you start to hear bubbles making noise (about 3 minutes). Remove from heat.

3. **Mash and blend the grape syrup.** Carefully (the pot is still hot!) mash the grapes with a potato masher or fork to get the juice out. Pour the grapes and hot liquid into a blender, then blend until smooth.

4. **Strain and chill the grape syrup.** Set a fine-mesh strainer over the medium mixing bowl. Pour the blended grapes into the strainer, use a wooden spoon to help press all the liquid through the strainer. Discard the grape pieces. Let syrup chill in fridge for at least 30 minutes, or up to 2 days in an airtight container.

5. **Serve.** Set out 6 glasses and add 4 ice cubes to each glass. Measure ½ cup grape syrup into each glass, then top off each glass with ½ cup soda water. 🖐 Garnish with a lemon wheel (see Quick Tip below) and serve right away.

Quick tip: Garnish each glass with a lemon wheel to make it look super festive: Wash 1 lemon. Slice it into round slices about ¼ inch thick. Use the knife to make a small cut from the edge to the middle of the lemon slice. Use that small cut to help the lemon wheel grip the rim of the glass.

Personalized Soda Straws

Make personalized grape soda straws for your pizza party guests. You'll need one straw for each guest, colored tape like washi tape or masking tape, scissors, and a permanent marker. First, tear a piece of tape three to four inches long. Next, wrap it around the straw about one inch from the top. Try to line it up so that the edges match each other. Cut a flag shape in the end of the tape. Write a guest's name on the tape with permanent marker. Repeat until all your guests have straws. Set each straw in an empty glass at the dinner table. Now your guests will know where to sit and can sip their grape soda in style!

A PIZZA MY HEART

SERVES **4 TO 6** PREP TIME: **30 MINUTES** COOK TIME: **15 MINUTES**

NUT-FREE, VEGETARIAN

TOOLS TO GATHER

Rimmed baking sheet

Mixing bowls

Plastic wrap

Dry measuring cups and spoons

Liquid measuring cup

Wooden spoon

Spoon

Pastry brush (or paper towel)

Wide spatula

Pizza cutter

Cutting board

INGREDIENTS TO HAVE

2 tablespoons **olive oil**, divided

1 tablespoon **granulated sugar**

1 tablespoon **active dry yeast**

2 cups **all-purpose flour**, divided

¾ teaspoon **salt**, divided

1 teaspoon **garlic powder**, divided

⅔ cup plus 2 tablespoons
    water, divided

6 ounces (⅔ cup) **tomato puree**

½ teaspoon **dried oregano**

⅛ teaspoon **black pepper**

1 cup **shredded mozzarella cheese**

Gather your guests in the kitchen for a recipe that everyone can help make. The pizza features a quick dough that rises in 15 minutes and is easy to shape into a crust (sorry, no tossing!). Bonus: Pals can pick and choose the toppings.

1. **Preheat the oven and prepare the pan.** 🖐 Preheat the oven to 450°F. Pour 1 tablespoon olive oil onto the baking sheet, then use the pastry brush or paper towel to coat the sheet with oil.

2. **Make the dough.** In large mixing bowl, pour in the sugar, active dry yeast, 1 cup all-purpose flour, ½ teaspoon salt, ½ teaspoon garlic powder. Stir to combine. Add ⅔ cup water, stir to combine. Add 2 more tablespoons water. Add 1 cup of all-purpose flour a little at a time, kneading it into the dough with your hands as you go. Cover with plastic wrap and let rise for 15 minutes.

3. **Make the sauce.** In a medium mixing bowl, stir tomato puree, dried oregano, ½ teaspoon garlic powder, ¼ teaspoon salt, and black pepper.

4. **Prepare the toppings.** Pour shredded cheese into a small bowl. Prepare any other optional toppings you're using.

5. **Stretch the dough.** Put the dough in the middle of the prepared baking sheet. Use your fingers to press the dough toward the pan edges, filling the whole pan. Try to make the dough an even thickness without any holes (see Kneading and Stretching Pizza Dough, page 78).

6. **Top the pizza**. Pour the sauce onto the dough, use a spoon to spread it evenly. Leave a 1-inch border around the edge with no sauce (for the crust). Sprinkle shredded cheese on top of sauce. Add optional toppings. Use a pastry brush or paper towel to coat the crust with 1 tablespoon olive oil.

7. **Bake the pizza.** Bake the pizza for 12 to 15 minutes, until the crust is golden brown and the cheese is bubbly.

8. **Serve.** Let the pizza cool for 5 minutes. Use a wide spatula to carefully transfer the pizza to a cutting board. Cut into 8 rectangles with a pizza cutter. Serve 1 to 2 rectangles per person.

Swap it: Guests with allergies can still join the fun! For a gluten or wheat allergy, look for gluten-free pizza crusts available at many grocery stores (check the freezer aisle), or use a gluten-free corn tortilla instead of crust. For vegan guests or a dairy allergy, leave the cheese off their part of the pizza or use vegan mozzarella-style shreds.

Kneading and Stretching Pizza Dough

Kneading (pronounced "needing") is the process of pressing and folding dough until it is smooth. Pizza dough has to be kneaded to create gluten, the protein that gives dough its structure. Here's how you do it.

ALL YOU KNEAD IS LOVE

Dust counter with flour and put dough on counter. The flour keeps the dough from sticking as you work with it. If your hands stick to the dough, try dusting them with a small bit of flour too.

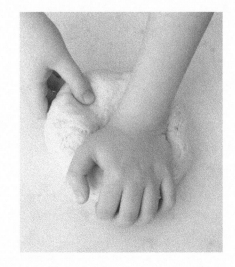

Press down and out. Use the heel of your hand to press the dough down and away from you.

Fold in half and press again. Fold the dough in half toward you and press down and away again.

Rotate and repeat. Turn the dough 45 degrees and repeat the same process (fold in half, press down and away).

Repeat until smooth. Keep kneading the dough until it is smooth. Some doughs require you to knead for 10 minutes, but for the A Pizza My Heart (page 76) dough, you can stop kneading when all of the flour is mixed in.

STRETCH IT OUT

Once your dough is kneaded and it's had time to rise, it's time to stretch it into the shape you want (in this case, pizza dough shape!) Here's how:

Keep it warm. Make sure the dough is at room temperature. If it's too cold, it will be much harder to stretch.

Oil the pan and hands. Brush the baking sheet and your hands with olive oil to keep dough from sticking.

Flatten into disc. Take your ball of dough and put it in the center of the baking sheet. Press down with your fingers to flatten the ball into a disc shape about 1 inch thick.

Stretch to fill baking sheet. Starting from the middle, use fingers to slowly press outward, making the dough wider and thinner a little at a time. If your dough isn't filling the entire baking sheet, find the thickest parts of the dough and gradually press them outward. Try to make the dough the same thickness on all parts of the pan. If you make any holes, just pinch the dough to seal them up.

Making a Pizza Together

Making pizza can be a fun party activity. Split your guests into three teams; each team is in charge of a different part of the recipe. Team 1 can make the dough, Team 2 can make the sauce, and Team 3 can prepare the toppings. Then the teams can come together and decorate the pizza as one. Put each topping into a separate small bowl to make it easier for your fellow chefs.

You can top a pizza with almost anything, but here are some of my favorites:

* Fresh basil (about ¼ cup basil leaves)

* Fresh oregano (about ¼ cup oregano leaves)

* Mushrooms (about 1 cup, stems removed, then thinly sliced)

* Pepperoni (as many as you like!)

* Sliced black or green olives (from a 2.25-ounce can, drained and rinsed)

RAINBOW FRUIT PIZZA

SERVES **6** PREP TIME: **20 MINUTES** COOK TIME: **20 MINUTES**

GLUTEN-FREE, NUT-FREE, VEGETARIAN

TOOLS TO GATHER

Baking sheet

Nonstick spray

Mixing bowls

Dry measuring cups and spoons

Spoons

Potato masher or fork

Cutting board

Chef's knife

Flexible spatula

Wide spatula

Pie cutter

INGREDIENTS TO HAVE

4 ripe **bananas**

1 cup **old-fashioned rolled oats**

⅓ cup **flaxseed meal** (or almond or whole-wheat flour)

4 tablespoons **honey**, divided

2 cups **plain Greek yogurt**

1 teaspoon **vanilla extract**

1 **clementine**

½ cup **green grapes**

½ cup **blueberries**

½ cup **raspberries**

There's never enough pizza, so surprise your guests with pizza for dessert! This rainbow deliciousness has a banana-oatmeal cookie crust, vanilla yogurt sauce, and colorful fruit topping. Prepare this pizza before your guests arrive so it has time to chill.

1. **Preheat the oven and prepare the pan.** Preheat the oven to 375°F. Spray the baking sheet with nonstick spray.

2. **Make the crust.** Peel 3 bananas and place in a large mixing bowl. With a potato masher or fork, mash the bananas until soft. Add old-fashioned rolled oats, flaxseed meal, and 3 tablespoons honey. Stir to combine.

3. **Bake the crust.** Pour the mixture onto the prepared baking pan. With a spoon, shape the crust into a circle about ½ inch thick. Bake for 20 minutes, until the crust can be lifted with a wide spatula (it will not be crispy).

CONTINUED

4. **Make the yogurt sauce.** In a medium mixing bowl, stir the Greek yogurt, vanilla extract, and 1 tablespoon honey until combined.

5. **Prepare fruit toppings.** Peel and separate the clementine into segments, removing strings. 🖐 Peel the remaining banana and cut into slices ¼ inch thick. 🖐 Cut each grape in half.

6. **Top the pizza.** 🖐 Let the crust cool for 5 minutes. Carefully use the wide spatula to peel the crust off the pan and transfer to the serving plate. With a flexible spatula, spread the yogurt sauce on top. Decorate with the fruit.

7. **Serve.** Chill the pizza for at least 15 minutes, or up to several hours. Keep refrigerated until ready to eat. Cut the pizza with the pie cutter into 6 pieces and serve with a fork.

Decorate: Decorate the pizza in rainbow circles! Start with red raspberries in the center, then make a circle of orange clementine slices, then yellow bananas, then green grapes, then blue blueberries. You can also substitute other colorful rainbow fruits like strawberry, pineapple, kiwi, or purple grapes, and make any pattern on the pizza that makes you smile.

CHAPTER 8
Hawaiian Luau

Grab your favorite surf shirt and transport your guests to the Hawaiian Islands with this luau-themed party! To set the mood, invite guests to wear big flowers, board shorts, or grass skirts, and play ukulele music on speakers when they arrive. Set the food out on a buffet table to keep the vibe as casual as an island breeze.

The Teriyaki Pineapple Kebabs (page 87) are best marinated overnight, so start that recipe the day before. Assemble kebab skewers just ahead of party time so you're not busy when guests arrive, and pop kebabs in the oven 30 minutes before you want to eat. Prepare the Coconut Cooler (page 86) just before your partygoers show up. Give them a true Hawaiian resort greeting and hand them drinks as they arrive. The Aloha Pineapple Pops (page 90) are frozen, so you can make them well ahead of the party and serve them for dessert.

COCONUT COOLER

SERVES **4** PREP TIME: **5 MINUTES**

DAIRY-FREE, GLUTEN-FREE, VEGETARIAN

TOOLS TO GATHER

Blender
Dry measuring cups
Liquid measuring cup
Paper umbrellas (optional)

INGREDIENTS TO HAVE

1 **ripe banana**
2 cups **frozen pineapple chunks**
1 (13.5-ounce) can **coconut milk**
1 cup **plain soymilk** (or milk
  of choice)
16 **ice cubes** (for serving)

One sip of this refreshing drink and your feet will start dancing a hula. Blend it up just before the luau starts and serve it to your guests when they arrive to set the mood. (Note: While coconuts are not actually nuts, some people who are allergic to nuts might also be allergic to coconuts, so be sure to ask your guests.)

1. **Prepare the banana and pineapple.** Peel the banana, break in half with your hands, and put in the blender. Add the frozen pineapple chunks.

2. **Add liquids.** Stir the coconut milk to combine coconut liquids and solids. Add the entire can of coconut milk to the blender. Add soymilk to the blender.

3. **Blend.** Turn the blender up to the highest speed and blend until completely combined.

4. **Serve.** Gather 4 cups and add 3 to 4 ice cubes to each. Pour 1 cup of the coconut cooler in each glass. Garnish with paper umbrella.

> **Quick tip:** To make cleanup a breeze, pour dish soap and water into the blender. Run the blender with soap and water for a minute or two. When you pour out the water, most of the food will come right out!

TERIYAKI PINEAPPLE KEBABS

SERVES 4 TO 6 PREP TIME: 30 MINUTES COOK TIME: 30 MINUTES

DAIRY-FREE, NUT-FREE, VEGETARIAN, VEGAN

TOOLS TO GATHER

Plates

Bowl

Cutting board

Chef's knife

Measuring spoons

Spoon

Resealable plastic bag

12 bamboo or metal skewers

Rimmed baking sheet

Pastry brush

INGREDIENTS TO HAVE

1 (14-ounce) package
  extra-firm tofu

1 **navel orange**

3 tablespoons **soy sauce**

2 teaspoons **sesame oil** (or
  olive oil)

1 teaspoon **garlic powder**

1 **bell pepper**

2 cups **fresh pineapple chunks**

1 (12-ounce) pint **cherry or
  grape tomatoes**

Luaus usually serve food made on a grill or over a fire pit. These kebabs have the same island flavors but without the fire. Assemble your colorful kebabs before the luau starts and bake them in an oven 30 minutes before mealtime.

1. **Preheat the oven, press the tofu.** Preheat the oven to 400°F. Line a plate with a clean kitchen towel and place the tofu on top of the towel. Place a second plate on top of the tofu, then place something heavy (like a pot or canned good) on top of the pile. This will squeeze extra water out of the tofu.

2. **Prepare the marinade.** Cut the orange in half and squeeze juice from both halves into a small mixing bowl. Add soy sauce, sesame oil, and garlic powder. Stir to combine.

3. **Marinate the tofu.** Cut the block of tofu into 32 tofu cubes. Place the cubes in a resealable plastic bag, pour half the marinade into the bag, and gently shake to coat. Save the rest of the marinade for later. If you have time, let the tofu marinate in the fridge for an hour or even overnight.

CONTINUED

4. **Slice the bell pepper and pineapple chunks.** Slice the bell pepper into strips (see How to Cut Bell Pepper and Onion, page 36). Cut each strip into a square about the same size as the tofu cubes. If any pineapple cubes are very large, cut them to be similar size to the tofu.

5. **Assemble the kebabs.** To make a kebab, take the skewer and carefully stab each piece of food in the center. For each kebab, add: 3 pieces of tofu, 2 tomatoes, 2 pineapple pieces, and 2 bell pepper pieces. Repeat until all ingredients are used up, making 10 to 12 kebabs. Place each kebab on a rimmed baking sheet. Cover with plastic wrap and refrigerate until ready to cook.

6. **Bake the kebabs.** Bake the kebabs for 30 minutes, until the tofu is firm to the touch.

7. **Serve.** With a pastry brush, brush the leftover marinade on both sides of each skewer. Serve kebabs fresh out of the oven or at room temperature.

Swap it: Tofu not your thing? Swap it with chicken instead. You'll need 1 pound of boneless, skinless chicken breasts. Cutting raw meat is tricky, so ask for a grown-up's help to cut the chicken into equal-size cubes. Follow the same instructions to make the marinade and to assemble the kebabs. Bake for 25 to 30 minutes at 400°F (until chicken is cooked through).

Juice Citrus Like a Pro

There are three different ways you can juice citrus fruit (lemon, limes, oranges, and grapefruit). No matter which kind you use, start the same way:

1. Before you cut the fruit, put it on the countertop, and press down as you roll it back and forth a few times. This will help more juice come out.

2. Cut the fruit in half, and use one of the methods below to get the juice.

WITH YOUR HANDS

The first way is the most low-tech: Use your hands! Depending on how much juice you need, this can get pretty tiring. If you're using a lemon or a seeded orange, learn this cool trick to keep the seeds from getting in your food. Cup your non-dominant hand and face it palm up. Squeeze the fruit over this hand. Your hand will catch the seeds, and the citrus juice will run over your hand and into the bowl. Press your thumb into the fruit to get even more juice out.

WITH A CITRUS REAMER

A citrus reamer is a cone-shaped tool with grooves that you use to juice citrus. It can either have a handle or sit on a table. Whichever kind you have, you'll press the cut citrus-half into the tip of the cone, then twist the fruit around and around. The grooves will help the juice come out and will catch a lot of the seeds, too.

WITH A CITRUS PRESS

A citrus press (sometimes called a citrus juicer) has two handles connected by a hinge. You'll need a large one to juice an orange, and a smaller one for lemons and limes. You put the citrus half in the bowl part and then squeeze the two handles toward each other. The juice comes out of small slots in the bowl, so the press catches the seeds.

ALOHA PINEAPPLE POPS

SERVES **6** PREP TIME: **25 MINUTES** FREEZER TIME: **30 MINUTES**

DAIRY-FREE, GLUTEN-FREE, VEGETARIAN

TOOLS TO GATHER

Microwave-safe bowl

Flexible spatula

Medium bowl

18 food-safe popsicle sticks
   or toothpicks

Serving tray or baking sheet

Wax or parchment paper

INGREDIENTS TO HAVE

2 cups **fresh pineapple cubes**

1 cup **dark chocolate chips**

1 cup **dried coconut flakes**

Hawaiians use the word "aloha" to mean both hello and goodbye. But once you serve these chocolate-covered pineapple pops to your friends at the luau, you will be getting a lot more hellos than goodbyes. (Note: While coconuts are not actually nuts, some people who are allergic to nuts might also be allergic to coconuts, so be sure to ask your guests.)

1. **Prepare the pineapple chunks.** Count 18 pineapple chunks and place on a clean kitchen towel. Place another kitchen towel on top and press down gently. Blotting the pineapple makes it dry enough for the chocolate to stick. Set aside.

2. **Melt the chocolate and prepare the coconut.** Pour the dark chocolate chips into a medium microwave-safe bowl. Microwave in 30-second bursts until chocolate chips are melted enough to stir together (1 to 3 minutes). Take out of microwave with oven mitts. Stir with a flexible spatula until smooth and set aside. Pour the coconut flakes into a second bowl.

3. **Assemble the pineapple pops.** Line a freezer-safe serving platter or baking sheet with wax or parchment paper. To make one pop: Stick a popsicle stick (or toothpick) in a pineapple chunk, dunk in chocolate until all sides are coated, then roll in coconut flakes until coconut covers chocolate. Place on the prepared platter. Repeat until you've

made 18 pops, using the flexible spatula for the chocolate when you get to the bottom of the bowl.

4. **Freeze the pops.** Put the pineapple pops in the freezer for at least 30 minutes.

5. **Serve.** Let thaw for at least 5 minutes before serving. Because they're frozen, they should be able to sit out at room temperature for at least an hour before they're too melted to eat.

Make ahead: You can make these pops well in advance, even weeks ahead of time if you really want! So they take up less space in your freezer, wait until they're completely frozen and then transfer to resealable plastic bags. Make 3 layers of pops with wax or parchment paper in between them so they won't stick together, then slide into the plastic bag.

Aloha Party Banner

Say "Aloha" to your party guests in style! You'll need five pieces of construction paper, a pencil, scissors, a long string, and a hole punch (optional). Write one letter on each piece of paper, spelling A-L-O-H-A with capital letters. If you're feeling that artistic flare, make the letter "O" in the shape of a pineapple! Punch two holes at the top of each letter, then string them on the string in order. Use removable tape like washi tape or painter's tape to tape the string to the wall behind the serving table or tie it to something like a curtain rod. If you have an extra grass skirt or two, tape that to the table edge to complete the look.

DIY Hula Leis

No luau is complete without flowered leis, so get everyone together to make your own! Gather straws, construction paper, string or yarn, scissors, and a hole punch (optional). To make flowers, fold a piece of construction paper into thirds. Cut flower shapes into the paper. Since the paper is folded in thirds, you'll make three flowers each time. Make six flowers for a bracelet or 18 for a necklace.

Use the hole punch to make a hole in the middle of the flowers, or close the scissors and carefully push the point through the paper to make a hole.

Cut one straw (for a bracelet) or three straws (for a necklace) into five pieces each. Cut a piece of string to the length you need for a bracelet or necklace. Make sure to give yourself enough string to tie it around your wrist or neck. Then thread a flower followed by a straw, and repeat until it's filled up.

CHAPTER 9
Ice Cream Social

You scream, I scream, we all scream for ice cream! Your guests will run to build their own ice cream sundaes at your ice cream–themed celebration. But the real cherry on top? Having a blast with your friends.

Cook the syrup for Strawberry Milk (page 96) up to two days before the party. Have the Trail Mix Cones (page 98) ready to set the stage when your guests arrive. Whip up the toppings for the Splendid Sundaes (page 99) right before setting up your sundae bar. Sundaes require audience participation, so invite your guests to add their own toppings. Strawberry milk is perfect to wash down sundaes.

STRAWBERRY MILK

SERVES **4** PREP TIME: **10 MINUTES** COOK TIME: **15 MINUTES**

GLUTEN-FREE, NUT-FREE, VEGETARIAN

TOOLS TO GATHER

Large stockpot
Dry measuring cups
Liquid measuring cup
Wooden spoon
Potato masher or fork
Fine-mesh strainer
Spoon
Mixing bowl

INGREDIENTS TO HAVE

2½ cups **frozen strawberries**
½ cup **granulated sugar**
2½ cups **water**
1 quart **milk** of choice

What could possibly make your ice cream sundae better? Scrumptious strawberry milk will amp it up. This milk (dairy, nut, or soy) is super strawberry-y because it is made with homemade strawberry syrup. You could even get wild and double the syrup recipe to use as a sundae topping!

1. **Combine the ingredients.** Add strawberries, sugar, and water to a large stockpot.

2. **Cook the strawberry syrup.** Heat stockpot over high heat and bring the water to boil. As soon as it begins to boil, reduce the heat to low and cook uncovered, stirring occasionally. Cook until the liquid reduces into a syrup, about 15 minutes. Remove from heat.

3. **Mash and strain the strawberries.** Use a potato masher or fork to mash the strawberries. Set a fine-mesh strainer over a medium mixing bowl. Carefully pour the syrup into the strainer. Use a spoon to push the syrup through the strainer.

4. **Serve.** Gather 4 glasses. Pour ¼ cup strawberry syrup into each cup, then pour 1 cup milk into each cup. Stir together with a spoon and serve.

Make ahead: You can make the strawberry syrup up to 2 days ahead. Store in the fridge in an airtight container. When you're ready to serve the strawberry milk, just mix it into the milk and enjoy. And don't forget your extra batch to serve with your Splendid Sundaes (page 99).

Ice Cream Cone Centerpieces

Gather brown construction paper or brown paper bags, a brown crayon or marker, tissue paper, scissors, and tape. Cut a 10-inch circle out of paper (it doesn't need to be perfectly round). To make a waffle cone pattern, draw lines going one direction and then in the opposite direction.

Roll the paper into a cone shape with the lines facing out, tape it in place.

Take one sheet of tissue paper and crumble it up into a ball shape. Tuck it into the cone. Make as many ice cream cones as you'd like, and then stick them in mason jars, clear glasses, or flower vases. Now you've created that true ice cream parlor setting!

TRAIL MIX CONES

SERVES **4 TO 6** PREP TIME: **15 MINUTES**

GLUTEN-FREE, VEGETARIAN

TOOLS TO GATHER

Large mixing bowl
Dry measuring cups
Wooden spoon
Muffin tin

INGREDIENTS TO HAVE

12 **wafer ice cream cones**
2 cups **nuts** of choice
1 cup **dried fruit**
2 cups **popped popcorn**
½ cup **dark chocolate chips**

Your guests can boost their energy as they trek to the sundae bar with this cone-themed appetizer. Served in ice cream cones, you can customize the trail mix to your liking by choosing the nuts and dried fruit you use in your mix.

1. **Prepare the cones.** Set the muffin tin on the counter. Stand up 1 ice cream cone in each muffin compartment, then set aside.

2. **Combine nuts and fruit.** Combine the nuts and fruit in large mixing bowl. If you're using multiple types of nuts or fruit, you can combine them any way you'd like. Just make sure that the amount adds up to 2 cups nuts and 1 cup dried fruit.

3. **Add the popcorn and chocolate.** Add the popcorn and chocolate to the large mixing bowl.

4. **Stir and fill the cones.** Use a wooden spoon to stir the trail mix together. Use your hands to put trail mix into all 12 cones and serve.

Swap it: If you have a guest with a nut allergy, swap the 2 cups mixed nuts with pretzel sticks or cereal. Make the cones vegan and dairy-free with dairy-free chocolate chips and unbuttered popcorn.

SPLENDID SUNDAES

SERVES 6 PREP TIME: 20 MINUTES

GLUTEN-FREE, NUT-FREE, VEGETARIAN

TOOLS TO GATHER

Electric mixer or stand mixer
Large freezer-safe bowl
Liquid measuring cup
Dry measuring cups and spoons
1-gallon freezer bag
Microwave-safe mixing bowl
Wooden spoon
Small bowls and spoons
Ice cream scoop

INGREDIENTS TO HAVE

1 cup **heavy whipping cream**
2 tablespoons **granulated sugar**
7 ounces **bittersweet baking chocolate**
2 tablespoons **virgin coconut oil**

Your Splendid Sundae bar features a one-two punch of homemade whipped cream and magic shell chocolate sauce. This "magic" sauce hardens within seconds to create a crunchy chocolatey shell. Serve your ice cream flavors with any other yummy toppings you'd like (fresh fruit, nuts, sprinkles, and marshmallows)!

1. **Chill the whipped cream tools.** Chill the large mixing bowl and electric mixer beaters (whisk shape if possible) in the freezer.

2. **Break the chocolate into small pieces.** Put the chocolate bars inside the gallon freezer bag and seal. Use hands to break up into smaller pieces about 1-inch wide. Pour into the microwave-safe medium mixing bowl.

3. **Melt the chocolate.** Microwave the chocolate for 30 seconds, take out and stir. Repeat microwaving for 30 seconds and stirring until the chocolate is melted (1 to 2 minutes of microwaving total).

4. **Add the coconut oil.** Pour the coconut oil onto the bowl of chocolate. The oil might be solid in the container. If so, use a spoon to scrape it out of the container. Stir until completely dissolved. The chocolate should easily drip from the spoon. Set aside for up to 30 minutes.

CONTINUED

5. **Make the whipped cream.** Take the mixing bowl and beaters out of freezer. Pour the heavy cream and sugar into the chilled bowl. Whip until the cream forms stiff peaks.

6. **Serve.** Set up your ice cream bar. Put out the magic shell chocolate sauce, whipped cream, and ice cream, plus any other toppings you're using. Each topping should have its own bowl and serving spoon, and the ice cream should have scoops. Set out bowls for your guests so they can build their own perfect sundaes!

Make ahead: You can make the whipped cream before the party but on the same day, and store in the fridge in an airtight container until ready to serve. You might need to whisk it a bit to make it fluffy again. The magic chocolate shell sauce needs to be made right before serving. Once it cools down to room temperature (after 30 to 45 minutes), its "magic" fades.

How to Make Whipped Cream

Sure, you *can* buy whipped cream at the grocery store, but once you taste homemade whipped cream you will never go back! Here's how to do it.

INGREDIENTS
Make sure you are using "heavy *whipping* cream," not "heavy cream." You can also add all sorts of flavoring if you'd like: citrus juice, vanilla or almond extract, cocoa powder, and more.

KEEP IT CHILLY

In order for the cream to whip, *everything* you're using needs to be cold. Make sure your heavy whipping cream stays in the fridge until the moment you're ready to use it (and is not warm from the trip home from the grocery store).

Put your mixing bowl and whisk attachment or beaters in the freezer for at least 15 minutes before you start making whipped cream, and take them out just before you start.

USE THE RIGHT TOOLS

If you have a stand mixer, it makes whipping cream easy as pie (and delicious *with* pie, too!). Use the whisk attachment and set the mixer to the fastest setting, and you should have whipped cream in about 2 minutes.

Electric hand mixers are also great for making whipped cream. If yours comes with a whisk attachment, use that. If not, the regular beaters are also fine. Be patient; depending on how powerful your mixer is, it could take up to 10 minutes to make whipped cream.

It is possible to make whipped cream with just a whisk and your muscle power, but it is pretty tiring and takes a while. Have a teammate or two help you and take turns.

LOOK FOR "STIFF PEAKS"

When you're making whipped cream, you'll want to keep whipping until you see "stiff peaks." You have stiff peaks if, when lifting the mixture with a spoon, it stays totally pointy and does not droop. Here's what those look like!

Ice Cream Toss

Challenge your guests to a sweet game of ice cream toss! Gather a shallow cardboard box, 10 wafer cones, craft glue, and 10 large marshmallows (or Ping-Pong balls). Assemble your toss target before the party. Flip the box upside down and place the cones in a pyramid shape (one cone in the first row, two in the second, three in the third, and four in the fourth). Glue the cones to the box and let dry for a few minutes. Decorate the box with paint, markers, or stickers if you're feeling it!

   When it's time for the party, use pillows or a sheet to mark a start line on the floor about two feet away from the front of the box. Put 10 marshmallows in a bowl. Each contestant stands behind the line and tries to land a marshmallow inside as many ice cream cones as they can. The person with the most marshmallows in a cone wins!

CHAPTER 10
Summer Potluck

A potluck is where all your guests bring a dish to share. This one is geared toward summer, but a potluck is fun no matter the season or reason! For this one, turn the music up, gather your best outdoor games, and get ready for some fun in the sun.

All the dishes for this party can be made beforehand so you can spend your time outside with your buds! The Petite Peach Pies (page 109) can be made the day before and the Corn on the Cob Boats (page 107) can be started then, too. The Razzle Dazzle Iced Tea (page 106) should be prepped at least three hours before, so it can chill in the fridge before serving. Give yourself 30 minutes before the party starts to finish the corn boats and you'll have little to do once your guests arrive. Just set your table with your pies, corn cobs, iced tea, and an ice bucket, and get excited to taste the food everyone else brings!

RAZZLE DAZZLE ICED TEA

SERVES 4 PREP TIME: 20 MINUTES CHILL TIME: 3 HOURS

DAIRY-FREE, GLUTEN-FREE, NUT-FREE, VEGETARIAN

Tools to Gather

Large stockpot with lid
Dry measuring cups
Liquid measuring cup
Wooden spoon
Small bowl
Cutting board
Chef's knife
Kitchen tongs
Heat-safe pitcher or bowl

Ingredients to Have

4 cups **water**
¼ cup **granulated sugar**
¾ cup **fresh raspberries**
1 **lemon**
4 bags **decaffeinated black tea**
16 **ice cubes** (for serving)

This tea will refresh your potluck guests! The raspberries do double duty: They taste delicious and look awesome. Make it a few hours ahead so it has time to chill for a hot day.

1. **Boil.** Pour the water and sugar into the large stockpot. Bring to a boil over high heat.

2. **Prepare the fruit.** Meanwhile, pour the raspberries into the small bowl. Cut a lemon in half and squeeze the juice from 1 half into the bowl with the raspberries.

3. **Steep the tea.** When the water comes to a boil, turn off the heat and stir to dissolve the sugar. Pour the raspberries and lemon juice into the stockpot. Add 4 tea bags to the pot and cover with the lid. Steep for 3 to 4 minutes (follow the instructions on the tea box).

4. **Chill the tea.** When the tea has finished steeping, use kitchen tongs to remove the tea bags. Carefully pour tea into the heat-safe pitcher or bowl. Cover and chill in the fridge for at least 3 hours. Transfer to the pitcher and serve with a full ice bucket.

Make ahead: This tea needs at least 3 hours in the fridge before it will be cold, so plan ahead! But you shouldn't make it more than 8 hours in advance of serving because bacteria can start to grow in the tea (gross!).

CORN ON THE COB BOATS

SERVES 6 PREP TIME: 20 MINUTES COOK TIME: 20 MINUTES

GLUTEN-FREE, NUT-FREE, VEGETARIAN

Tools to Gather

Mixing bowl

Dry measuring cups and spoons

Liquid measuring cup

Chef's knife

Cutting board

Fork

Baking sheet

Aluminum foil

Ingredients to Have

6 **ears of corn**

⅓ cup **olive oil**

1 cup **crumbled feta cheese**

2 teaspoons **ground cumin**

2 teaspoons **sweet paprika**

1 teaspoon **garlic powder**

1 teaspoon **salt**

2 **limes**

These "boat" vessels make eating messy corn a little less messy! Aluminum foil boat hulls catch drips, making cobs easy to hold. Plus, they're cool. Watch as they float into your guests' mouths!

1. **Preheat the oven and prepare the corn.** Preheat the oven to 425°F. Peel off the corn husks and the silky strings. Break off the end of the cob. To break the corn in half, use a chef's knife to mark a line in the kernels at the center of the corn (don't try to cut all the way through the cob). Put one hand on each side of the cut, then press apart to break the corn.

2. **Mix the cheesy corn spice.** Pour the olive oil into the medium mixing bowl. Add the feta to the bowl. Add cumin, paprika, garlic powder, and salt to the bowl. Cut the limes in half and squeeze the juice from all 4 halves into the bowl. Use a fork to mash the cheese and mix until combined.

3. **Coat the corn and wrap in foil.** Tear 12 pieces of aluminum foil wide enough that they will go around a piece of corn. Roll a cob in the spicy cheese mix until all the sides are coated, then place in the center of one of the foil pieces. Scoop about 2 teaspoons of the cheese chunks from the mixture on top of the corn, then wrap the foil around the corn until it closes. Repeat for all 12 corn pieces. Place on a baking sheet with the foil openings facing up.

CONTINUED

4. **Bake.** 🤚 Bake for 20 minutes.

5. **Serve.** Let cool for at least 5 minutes before touching the foil. Slowly peel back the foil on top, but leave the foil around the bottom. Pinch the sides of the foil at the end of the corn to make boat holders so guests can easily pick up the corn. Serve warm or at room temperature.

Make ahead: You can prep these boats the day before the party. Follow steps 1 to 3, then put the foil-wrapped corn in an airtight container in the fridge. When it's party time, bake them and serve. These cobs are extra delicious if eaten while still warm, but they are safe to be left at room temperature for up to 2 hours (shorter if it's hot outside!).

Make Your Corn Boats Shipshape

To create sailboats out of your corn boats, they need sails! Gather paper, toothpicks, tape, scissors, and markers. Cut 12 triangle sails out of the paper. Use markers to decorate them however you'd like! Flip over the sails so the decorated side is facedown. Place a toothpick at the bottom of each sail and use a piece of tape to secure them. When you're ready to serve your corn, push a sail into the top of each cob and arrange on a tray. If you have blue construction paper, you can put that on the serving tray and draw waves and fish on it too. Bon voyage!

PETITE PEACH PIES

SERVES **6** PREP TIME: **30 MINUTES** COOK TIME: **25 MINUTES**

DAIRY-FREE, NUT-FREE, VEGETARIAN

TOOLS TO GATHER

Nonstick spray

Muffin tin

Chef's knife

Cutting board

Mixing bowls

Dry measuring cups and spoons

Coffee mug

Rolling pin

Pastry brush

Butter knife

Fork

Spoon

Resealable plastic bag

Flexible spatula

INGREDIENTS TO HAVE

3 **ripe peaches**

2 tablespoons **dark brown sugar**

1 teaspoon **cinnamon**

1 pre-made **pie dough**

All-purpose flour (for dusting)

1 **egg**

2 **tablespoons water**

1 tablespoon **granulated sugar**
  (for dusting)

3 **graham crackers**

No need to share when everyone has their own personal pie! Celebrate delicious summer peaches with this simple pie filling (or substitute plums, nectarines, or apricots if you prefer). Top off these mini delights with vanilla ice cream or homemade whipped cream.

1. **Preheat the oven, prepare the pan.** Preheat the oven to 400°F. Spray 6 compartments of the muffin tin with nonstick spray.

2. **Make the pie filling.** Chop large chunks off 3 peaches, cutting around the pit. Place these chunks flat-side down. Medium dice by slicing strips ½-inch wide, then slicing the other direction to make cubes ½-inch wide. Measure 1½ cups of diced peaches, then pour into the medium mixing bowl. Add the dark brown sugar and cinnamon to the mixing bowl, stir to combine.

3. **Cut out the pie crusts.** Place one crust on a dry cutting board. Use the top of a coffee mug and a butter knife to trace 4 circles in the dough. Peel away the extra, roll it into a ball, then roll out to be the same thickness as the other circles. Trace 2 more circles and peel away the extra.

4. **Egg wash the crusts.** Dust the rolling pin with the all-purpose flour, then roll out the circles until they're a bit bigger. Crack the egg into a small bowl and add 2 tablespoons water. Beat the egg with a fork until combined. Use a pastry brush to

CONTINUED

paint each crust with this egg wash. Put about 1 tablespoon sugar in a second small bowl. Sprinkle a few pinches of sugar on top of each crust.

5. **Assemble the petite pies.** Press each crust into a muffin tin slot, with the egg washed side face down in the tin. Make crumbs with graham crackers (see How to Crumble, page 112). Pour ½ tablespoon of graham crumbs into the bottom of each crust. Divide about ¼ cup pie filling (including the juice) into each crust on top of the graham crumbs.

6. **Bake.** Bake for 25 minutes.

7. **Serve.** Let cool for 5 minutes. Very carefully, use a flexible spatula to scoop under the pie crusts and transfer them to the serving plate. Serve with optional ice cream or whipped cream.

Quick tip: This recipe works best with ripe peaches. Unripe peaches are very hard and don't budge at all when you squeeze them gently. When you squeeze a peach and it squishes a lot, it's ready! If peaches are not in season, you can also make this recipe with apples.

Bean Bag Toss

To play, you'll need teams of two, one referee, and one bean bag (or ball) per team. Players start by lining up in two lines about three feet apart, with partners facing each other. When the referee shouts "toss," the first partner gently tosses the bean bag to the other. If the bean bag is caught, the team moves onto the next round. If it's dropped, that team is out. At the beginning of each round, each team still left in the game takes a step backwards, making it harder for the next round. The game ends when a single winning team still stands. Try it with water balloons, too!

How to Crumble

Sometimes recipes will call for "graham cracker crumbs" or for chocolate to be broken into small pieces before melting or baking. Wondering how to do that without making a huge mess in your kitchen? I've got you covered.

You'll need a resealable plastic bag that's bigger than the ingredient you're crumbling. Put the ingredient in the bag, and seal it while you squeeze out as much air as you can. Then, grab something heavy to help you crumble. Some great heavy tools are a rolling pin, a heavy canned good (like a can of beans), or a meat tenderizer. If you use a meat tenderizer, you'll want to use the flat sides. (The pointy side will poke a hole in your bag!)

Put the plastic bag down on the counter, then pound with your heavy object over and over. Follow the recipe's instructions to know how much pounding to do; if it tells you to make crumbs you'll want to keep going until the pieces are very small and the same size.

CHAPTER 11
Backyard Campout

If you have a backyard, you can have an outdoor adventure! Just grab a tent, or forage for blankets and fort-building materials in the house. For this party, you'll make traditional camping food but within the comforts of your own kitchen. Eat quickly to keep the bears away (just kidding!).

Prepare the In-Tents-ly Delicious Hamburger patties (page 117) before your guests arrive, then bake 15 minutes before dinner time. Leave your friends with a ghost story cliff-hanger while you head inside to make the Indoor S'mores (page 121) and start mulling the Campfire Cider (page 116). Eat the s'mores for dessert, then sip the cider to stay warm after the sun sets.

CAMPFIRE CIDER

SERVES **4 TO 6** PREP TIME: **5 MINUTES** COOK TIME: **25 MINUTES**

DAIRY-FREE, GLUTEN-FREE, NUT-FREE, VEGETARIAN

TOOLS TO GATHER

Large stockpot
Measuring spoons
Chef's knife
Cutting board
Fine-mesh strainer
Heat-safe mixing bowl
Ladle

INGREDIENTS TO HAVE

1 **navel orange**
6 **cinnamon sticks**
1 heaping teaspoon **whole cloves**
½ gallon **apple cider**

This hot mulled cider will give you the warm and cozies, even if you're sitting around a pretend campfire. Combine apple cider with orange, cinnamon, and cloves, and you've transformed an everyday drink into a delicious campout treat.

1. **Make the flavoring.** Slice the orange into slices ¼ inch thick and place in the large stockpot. Add the cinnamon sticks and cloves to the stockpot.

2. **Bring the cider to a boil.** Pour the ½ gallon apple cider into the stockpot. Put on the stove over high heat, bringing the cider to a boil (when large bubbles form on the surface of the cider).

3. **Simmer and strain.** Once the pot starts to boil, bring the cider to a simmer by reducing the heat to low. Simmer for 20 minutes. Set a fine-mesh strainer over a large heat-safe mixing bowl. At the end of 20 minutes, carefully pour the cider into the strainer.

4. **Serve.** Let cool for 7 to 10 minutes before serving. Use a ladle to scoop cider into 4 mugs. Garnish by floating one of the orange slices on top of the cider.

Swap it: There are many ways to make hot mulled cider. Just swap out cinnamon, cloves, and orange for other ingredients like sliced lemon, sliced ginger root, star anise, ground nutmeg, and whole allspice.

IN-TENTS-LY DELICIOUS HAMBURGERS

SERVES 4 PREP TIME: 15 MINUTES COOK TIME: 20 MINUTES

GLUTEN-FREE, NUT-FREE

TOOLS TO GATHER:

2 rimmed baking sheets

Metal cooling rack

Mixing bowls

Measuring spoons

Spoon

Butter knife

Wide spatula

2 cutting boards

Chef's knife

Instant-read
thermometer (optional)

INGREDIENTS TO HAVE

4 **hamburger buns** (gluten-free
or whole-wheat)

1 teaspoon **garlic powder**

1 teaspoon **onion powder**

1 teaspoon **salt**

½ teaspoon **black pepper**

1 pound **80-percent-lean
ground beef**

2 tablespoons **plain Greek yogurt**

4 **slices cheese** (optional)

1 **beefsteak tomato** (optional)

1 **red onion** (optional)

1 head **lettuce** (optional)

Hamburgers are classic campout food. No one has to know you've made these in an oven instead of over an open fire. Set up a burger topping bar with items like lettuce, ketchup, mustard, and pickles.

1. **Preheat the oven, prepare the pans.** Preheat the oven to 425°F. Open the hamburger buns and place facedown on the baking sheet. Place the metal cooling rack (what you'd use to cool cookies) on top of the second rimmed baking sheet.

2. **Make the seasoning blend.** In a small bowl, mix together the garlic powder, onion powder, salt, and pepper.

3. **Mix the beef.** Put the beef into the medium mixing bowl. Add the Greek yogurt, combine with hands. Form the beef into a circle with even thickness. Use a butter knife to divide into 4 equal quarters by drawing a plus sign in the circle.

4. **Make the burger patties.** Pick up one of the quarters, roll into a meatball, then flatten on a cutting board. Repeat for remaining quarters. Use fingers to press the burgers until they're all the same size and thickness, about 4½ to 5 inches wide and ½ inch thick.

CONTINUED

5. **Season and place on the rack.** Sprinkle the seasoning blend on one side of the burger until covered. Carefully flip over with the wide spatula, then season the other side. Place the burger on the cooling rack. Repeat for the remaining 3 burgers.

6. **Bake.** Bake burgers about 15 minutes for medium done, about 18 minutes for medium-well done, or 22 minutes for well done (see How to Cook a Hamburger, page 119). At 2 minutes left in your cook time, put the pan with the hamburger buns in the oven. If you're opting to make any of the patties into cheeseburgers, take the burgers out with 2 minutes left on your timer. Top with one cheese slice, returning to the oven for the last 2 minutes of cook time.

7. **Serve.** Set up a burger buffet by placing the burgers on one plate and buns on another. Set out tomatoes and onions, and any other toppings you dream of.

Quick tip: Make your hamburgers more exciting with toppings! While burgers are cooking, cut tomato slices and onion rings. Use the second cutting board so you don't contaminate them with the meat. (see How to Cut Bell Peppers and Onions, page 36 and How to Cut Tomatoes, page 48). Separate leaves from the head of lettuce, wash, and dry with a clean kitchen towel.

How to Cook a Hamburger

Cooking beef can be hard because you have options. Unlike chicken or turkey, where you always want to cook it all the way through so you kill all the germs, people eat beef cooked to different levels of doneness depending on how they like it. Here's a guide:

HOW DO YOU LIKE YOUR BURGER?

At a restaurant, have you ever heard a server ask, "How do you want your burger cooked?" The server is asking how much you'd like your burger to be cooked: medium, medium-well, or well done (never "rare" for food safety reasons).

Medium burgers are brown on the outside with lots of pink inside, and when you insert an instant-read thermometer into one, it will read 140 to 145°F.

Medium-well burgers are brown on the outside with a little pink inside, and when you insert an instant-read thermometer into one, it will read 150 to 155°F.

Well done burgers are brown inside and out, and when you insert an instant-read thermometer into one, it will read 160° F.

HOW TO CHECK A BURGER'S TEMPERATURE

The easiest way to check a burger's internal temperature is with an instant-read thermometer. To do this, take the pan out of the oven. Very carefully (the pan will be hot!), slide the thermometer in one side of the burger. You'll want to make sure the tip of the thermometer is in the middle of the patty; if it touches the pan or pokes out into the air it won't give an accurate reading. Even though it's an "instant" thermometer, wait until the reading stops changing, which will take about 20 seconds.

INDOOR S'MORES

SERVES **4 TO 6** PREP TIME: **15 MINUTES** COOK TIME: **1 MINUTE**

NUT-FREE, VEGETARIAN

TOOLS TO GATHER

Cutting board
Chef's knife
2 baking sheets
Kitchen tongs

INGREDIENTS TO HAVE

12 **large marshmallows**
8 **strawberries**
2 **bananas**
12 **graham crackers**
6 (1.5 ounce) **milk chocolate bars**

You can't have a campout without s'mores, but you can have s'mores without a campfire! The marshmallows are cooked with your oven's broil setting so they have the same toasty goodness as outdoor s'mores. The banana and strawberry slices make this dessert so yummy you'll be begging for s'more!

1. **Preheat the oven, prepare the marshmallows.** Set an oven rack to the second highest position. Turn your oven to the "broil" setting (high broil if you have that option). Arrange marshmallows on a baking sheet. Stand them on their flat end and group them close together in the middle of the baking sheet (so they'll all cook at the same speed). Set aside.

2. **Slice the bananas and strawberries.** Peel the bananas and cut off the ends. Slice them into ¼-inch-thick slices until you have 24 banana slices. Cut the leaf ends off 8 strawberries. Slice strawberries into ¼-inch-thick slices until you have 24 strawberry slices.

3. **Assemble the s'mores.** Break the graham crackers in half. Place 12 halves on a second baking sheet, set aside the rest for later. Break the chocolate bars in half. Place one half on top of each graham cracker. Place 2 strawberry slices and 2 banana slices on top of each chocolate piece.

CONTINUED

4. **Toast the marshmallows.** ✋ Turn on the oven light and put the baking sheet with the marshmallows on the high oven rack. Watch through the oven door and take them out of the oven when they start to turn brown on top (about 30 seconds). Marshmallows will go from toasted to burnt very quickly, so watch carefully! Take the pan out of the oven, flip over the marshmallows with kitchen tongs, then repeat to toast the other side.

5. **Finish the s'mores.** Place a toasted marshmallow on top of each prepared s'more. Take the remaining graham cracker halves and smush the marshmallows down.

6. **Serve.** Serve right away while the marshmallows are still warm.

Quick tip: The "broil" setting on ovens cooks food with very high heat and is sort of like cooking food over a grill or fire. Broilers are located in different places in different ovens, so it's best to ask your grown-up. If you can broil food in the main compartment of your oven, follow the instructions in steps 1 and 4. If your oven's broiler is in a drawer underneath the main oven, bake the marshmallows at 350°F for 4 to 6 minutes instead of broiling.

Make a Campground

Create your own trailhead! You'll need a cardboard box, scissors, packing or duct tape, markers, and a yard stick. Cut a rectangle out of cardboard, then write the name of your camp on it. Cut out a few long rectangles with an arrow point at the end of them. On each rectangle, write the names of national parks, lakes, mountains, neighborhood street names, whatever you'd like! Add the distance to these destinations (look up real distances online if you'd like). Tape the signs to a yard stick (or something else sturdy and long, like a gardening stake). Stick the yard stick in the ground for an authentic campground look!

Campfire Games

There are so many fun games you can play around a real (or imagined) campfire. Sit in a circle with your guests and try these.

TELEPHONE
The first person thinks of a sentence and whispers it to the person next to him or her. The sentence gets passed around the circle until it comes back to the original person. The original person shares with the group to laugh at how different the message has become.

THE ANIMAL GAME
The first person says the name of an animal. The next person has to think of an animal whose first letter is the same as their friend's animal's last letter. For example: Player 1 (Octopu**s**), Player 2 (**S**har**k**), Player 3 (**K**angaroo). Whoever can't think of an animal is out. Keep going until there's only one player left!

I WENT TO THE STORE
The first person says: "I went to the store and got a ___." Then the next person repeats what the first person said and adds something. For example: Player 1: "I went to the store and got a car." Player 2: "I went to the store and got a car and a pizza." Whoever makes a mistake is eliminated. Keep going until there is a winner!

CHAPTER 12
Birthday Bash

Happy birthday to you! It's time to celebrate another trip around the sun, and these colorful foods are perfect for partying. Set up the drinks, snacks, and cake on a buffet so your guests can grab a bite in between party activities.

Every part of the menu can be made ahead of time because you can't miss any part of this celebration of you. Make the dip for the Veggie Cups (page 128) up to three days ahead of time, and bake the layers for the Confetti Birthday Cake (page 130) up to two days before. Prepare the Fruit Water (page 126) the day before to give the fruit time to soak into the water. The day of the party, make the icing for the cake and put it together. Just before the party starts, slice the veggies for the Veggie Cups and assemble them.

FRUIT WATER

SERVES **6** PREP TIME: **15 MINUTES** CHILL TIME: **4 HOURS (OR OVERNIGHT)**

DAIRY-FREE, GLUTEN-FREE, NUT-FREE, VEGETARIAN

TOOLS TO GATHER

Cutting board
Chef's knife
Dry measuring cups
Liquid measuring cup
Pitcher

INGREDIENTS TO HAVE

1 cup **strawberries**
1 **navel orange**
½ cup **blueberries**
6 to 8 cups **water**

You may think water is boring now, but you'll change your mind after one sip of Fruit Water! By adding sliced fruit to water and letting it infuse for several hours in the fridge, your water will turn magically delicious. Chill for at least 4 hours, or overnight to make it extra flavorful.

1. **Slice the strawberries.** ✋ Cut off the stems of your strawberries. Cut each strawberry into slices about ¼ inch thick. When you have 1 cup of strawberry slices, pour into the pitcher.

2. **Slice the orange.** ✋ Cut off the ends of the orange. Slice the orange into slices about ¼ to ½ inch thick. Put the slices flat on the cutting board, then cut away the peel using straight cuts. Your orange should look like a hexagon when you're finished. Discard the peel, then put the orange slices in the pitcher.

3. **Slice the blueberries.** To cut blueberries, hold a blueberry with the bridge grip, and slide the knife underneath to cut. Cut each blueberry, then put in the pitcher.

4. **Add the water.** Measure 6 cups of water and pour into the pitcher. If your pitcher is large, you might be able to add more water.

5. **Chill.** Cover the top of the pitcher and chill the Fruit Water in the fridge for at least 4 hours, overnight is ideal.

6. **Serve.** Set out the pitcher with glasses.

Swap it: You can make Fruit Water with lots of different ingredients and flavors to give it a different flare! Pineapple gives it a taste of the tropics. Lemons or cucumbers bring a fresher taste. If you're using any citrus fruit, make sure to cut off the peel or else your water will taste bitter.

Say Cheese!

Take photobooth pictures so your guests will have a fun souvenir from your party! You'll need: an instant camera and film (or a smartphone), props, and a volunteer photographer. Before the party, gather props like wigs, masks, hats, crowns, feather boas, and whatever else you can find from your Halloween costume and dress-up clothes collection. You can also make signs that say things like "Happy Birthday!" or "[Name]'s 12th Birthday Bash." Set up the props and signs on a table near the backdrop. Finally, you'll need someone to take the photos (like a grown-up). Then you and your friends can pose in front of the backdrop and take pictures throughout the party. If you have an instant camera, the photos will print out right there and your guests can take them home. Or, you can use a smartphone to take pictures and print them with a printer before the guests leave or send them via email after the party.

VEGGIE CUPS

SERVES 6 PREP TIME: 25 MINUTES

GLUTEN-FREE, NUT-FREE, VEGETARIAN

TOOLS TO GATHER

Dry measuring cups and spoons
Mixing bowl
Spoon
Cutting board
Chef's knife
Toothpicks
Vegetable peeler
Juice glasses

INGREDIENTS TO HAVE

2 cups **plain Greek yogurt**
¼ cup **dried onion flakes**
1 teaspoon **onion powder**
½ teaspoon **garlic powder**
½ teaspoon **salt**
6 ounces **cherry or grape tomatoes**
2 **bell peppers**
4 **celery stalks**
3 large **carrots**

Eat the colors of the rainbow with these fun veggie cups! The vegetables stand front and center in cups with homemade onion dip at the bottom, so everyone can tote their own snack around the party. Customize these cups with other easy-to-dip vegetables like snow peas, broccoli, cucumbers, and green beans.

1. **Make the onion dip.** In a medium mixing bowl, combine the Greek yogurt, dried onion flakes, onion powder, garlic powder, and salt. Stir to combine and refrigerate until ready to serve.

2. **Put the tomatoes on the toothpicks.** Count out 6 toothpicks. Put 2 to 3 tomatoes on each toothpick, then set aside.

3. **Slice the celery stalks and the bell peppers.** Slice the white bottoms and leafy tops off the 4 celery stalks. Slice each stalk into pieces about 3 inches long. For pieces cut from the wide part of the stalk, you might want to cut them in half lengthwise (hotdog-style). Slice the bell peppers into strips about ½-inch wide.

4. **Peel and slice the carrots.** Peel 3 carrots and slice off their ends. Cut each carrot into pieces about 3 inches long. Cut each piece in half hotdog-style, place flat edge on cutting board. Cut each piece into strips about ½-inch wide.

5. **Assemble the veggie cups.** Measure about ⅓ cup onion dip and spoon into the bottom of 6 clear cups. Wipe up any dip dribble. Arrange your veggies in rainbow order around the outside of the cup like this: 1 tomato toothpick, 2 orange bell pepper strips, 2 yellow bell pepper strips, 2 celery sticks, 2 purple carrot sticks.

6. **Serve.** Set out the cups on a serving tray. If they'll be sitting out for a while, put ice cubes on the serving tray to keep the dip cold.

Make ahead: You can make the onion dip up to 3 days ahead of time, as long as you store it in an airtight container and keep it in the fridge. Wait until just before the party to cut your veggies, though, because they'll dry out if you do it ahead of time.

Make a Photobooth Backdrop

This colorful backdrop is perfect for a photobooth or to put behind a buffet table. Gather crepe paper, masking tape, and scissors, and find an empty wall. Cut 10 to 15 pieces of crepe paper that are about as tall as you are. Use masking tape to tape the first piece to the wall about two feet above your head. Twist the crepe paper until it makes a spiral shape, then tape the bottom to the wall. Repeat for the rest of the pieces of crepe paper. You can space them out or make them close together depending on how big your wall is. Make a pattern with different colors or use all the same color; it will look great either way!

CONFETTI BIRTHDAY CAKE

MAKES 12 SLICES PREP TIME: **40 MINUTES** COOK TIME: **30 MINUTES**

NUT-FREE, VEGETARIAN

TOOLS TO GATHER

Nonstick spray
9-inch cake pans
Mixing bowls
Dry measuring cups and spoons
Liquid measuring cup
Whisk
Flexible spatula
Electric mixer or stand mixer
Chef's knife
Offset spatula
Birthday candles
Matches or candle lighter
Pie server

INGREDIENTS TO HAVE

1½ cups **granulated sugar**
1 teaspoon plus pinch **salt,** divided
3 teaspoons **baking powder**
¼ cup **cornstarch**
2½ cups **all-purpose flour**
4 **eggs**
1 tablespoon plus 1 teaspoon
vanilla extract, divided
¾ cup plus 2 tablespoons
   milk, divided
1 cup **oil** (like canola, sunflower,
   or avocado)
½ cup **rainbow sprinkles**, plus
   more for decorating
1 cup (2 sticks) **unsalted butter**
2½ cups **confectioner's sugar**

For your special day, dive into this confetti cake topped with fluffy vanilla buttercream icing! Make the cake layers 2 days ahead of time (store at room temperature in airtight container) and assemble it and make the icing the day of the party. To make it birthday song–worthy, add sprinkles and birthday candles on top.

1. **Preheat the oven, prepare the pans.** 🤚 Preheat the oven to 350°F. Spray two 9-inch round cake pans with nonstick spray.

2. **Mix the dry ingredients.** In a large mixing bowl, combine sugar, 1 teaspoon salt, baking powder, cornstarch, and all-purpose flour. Whisk to combine thoroughly.

3. **Beat the wet ingredients.** Separate the egg whites into a small bowl, discard the yolks. In a medium mixing bowl, combine the egg whites, 1 tablespoon vanilla extract, ¾ cup milk, and oil. Beat with the whisk to combine.

4. **Combine the bowls, fold in the sprinkles.** Pour the wet ingredients into the dry ingredients. Beat with the whisk until thoroughly combined. Add the rainbow sprinkles, gently fold into the batter using the flexible spatula.

5. **Bake.** Divide the batter evenly between the prepared cake pans. 🤚 Bake for 28 to 32 minutes, until a toothpick inserted into the center of the cakes comes out clean. Let cool completely before icing.

6. **Make the icing.** In a large mixing bowl, add butter softened to room temperature (microwave about 10 seconds if coming from fridge). Add sugar, 1 teaspoon vanilla extract, 2 tablespoons milk, and a pinch of salt. Use an electric mixer or stand mixer to cream into icing.

7. **Assemble the cake.** Use the flexible spatula to loosen the edges of the cakes, then turn the pans upside down onto the cutting board and hit the pan to get the layers out. 🖐 On a cutting board, use a chef's knife to cut away the brown edges around the outside of the cakes (to make the sprinkles show). Assemble and ice the cake (see A Piece of Cake!, page 132).

8. **Serve.** Arrange birthday candles on the cake and 🖐 light them. After singing, use the pie cutter to cut the cake into 12 slices (see A Piece of Cake!, page 132).

Quick tip: There's an easy way to separate egg whites from egg yolks. Crack the egg over a small bowl. Separate the shell into two pieces, letting the whites (the clear part) fall into the bowl but holding the yolk with one of the shell halves. Gently pour the yolk back and forth between the two shell halves a few times, each time letting the white drip into the bowl underneath.

A Piece of Cake!

BUILDING A LAYER CAKE

Make sure your cake layers are completely cooled. Place the first cake layer on your serving platter or cake stand. Use an offset spatula, which is a long skinny spatula with a crinkle in it that makes icing easier (or use a flexible spatula if you don't have one). Dollop half of the icing into the center of the layer. Spread it outward using the offset spatula, making sure that the icing is thick around the edges of the layer. Place the second cake layer on top and repeat with the second half of the icing. Since this top icing will be visible, make it look nice by spreading with circular strokes.

For the Confetti Birthday Cake recipe (page 130), you're making a "naked" cake, which means that you're not putting icing on the sides of the cake so you can see the confetti inside! For a regular cake, make more buttercream icing and ice the sides with an offset spatula, too.

DECORATING A CAKE

There are many ways to decorate a cake besides birthday candles. An easy decorating idea is to add sprinkles, covering the entire top or making a ring around the outside. You can write "Happy Birthday, [name]!" with gel icing on the top. Practice on a cutting board first before writing on the actual cake because it's hard to undo.

SERVING A CAKE

It's easiest to serve a cake with a pie cutter, which is a special triangle-shaped spatula. A 9-inch round cake should serve around 12 people. Use the pie cutter to make a cut from one edge to the center of the cake. Then, make a cut about 90° from that cut (so now you've made a slice that's a quarter of the cake). Divide that piece into three equal pieces, cutting from the center to the edge. Repeat three more times to serve all 12 slices.

To get the pieces out, slide the pie cutter underneath the slice. Quickly move it to the plate and tip it on its side. You might have to use your second hand to balance it. Getting the first piece of cake out is the hardest! If it crumbles, make that piece yours so your guests can all have a nice-looking piece of cake.

CHAPTER 13
Halloween
Boo-ffet

Invite your ghosts—I mean guests—to come dressed in their Halloween best. This Halloween Boo-ffet features a snack spread so awesomely Halloween-y you'll have to fight off the monsters trying to snatch it!

Make all the components for the Graveyard Dirt Cups (page 141) and the kiwi syrup for the Witches' Brew (page 136) up to 2 days in advance. Just before the party starts, make the Spider Bites (page 138), combine the kiwi syrup with soda water, and assemble the dirt cups. Set everything out on a spooky buffet table so guests can enjoy when they arrive.

WITCHES' BREW

SERVES 6 PREP TIME: 15 MINUTES

DAIRY-FREE, GLUTEN-FREE, NUT-FREE,
VEGETARIAN

TOOLS TO GATHER

Small stockpot

Dry and liquid measuring cups

Chef's knife

Cutting board

Spoon

Blender

Wooden spoon

Large serving bowl

Ladle

INGREDIENTS TO HAVE

1 liter unflavored **soda water**

½ cup **granulated sugar**

1 cup **water**

8 ripe **kiwi fruit**

24 **ice cubes** (for serving)

Those who are brave enough to try this spooky witches' brew will be rewarded with a frighteningly good kiwi soda. You can make it ahead of the party so you'll have plenty of time to mix with the other monsters!

1. **Chill the soda water, make the simple syrup.** Put the soda water in the fridge. ✋ Bring the sugar and water to a boil. Once boiling, turn off the heat and stir to dissolve the sugar. This is called "simple syrup."

2. **Cut and blend the kiwis.** ✋ Cut the kiwi fruit in half. Use a spoon to scoop the flesh out of the skin. Put in the blender, then blend until smooth.

3. **Stir.** Pour the kiwi puree into the simple syrup, then stir to combine.

4. **Add the soda water.** Pour the kiwi syrup into the large serving bowl. Pour the entire liter of soda water over the kiwi syrup. Stir to combine.

5. **Serve.** Serve with the ladle so guests can scoop out the witches' brew into cups. Set out the ice bucket.

Make ahead: You can make the kiwi syrup up to 2 days before the party. Just store the syrup in an airtight container until you're ready to serve and combine with the soda water right before the party starts.

Boo-tify Your Boo-ffet

There are lots of ways to creep out your ghost guests
by Halloween-ifying your buffet:

* Put down a black or orange tablecloth and stretch apart
  cotton batting or balls to look like spider webs (or tape white
  yarn to the tablecloth in a web pattern).

* Place plastic spiders on the webs (or make your own out
  of paper!).

* Cut bats out of black construction paper and stick to the wall
  with masking, painter, or washi tape.

* Add a jack-o'-lantern with an electric candle inside, or
  uncarved mini pumpkins to the table.

* Carve a small pumpkin and place a bowl in it to serve dip.

* Make edible "pumpkin" decor: Peel clementines and stick a
  celery stick in the top.

* Make edible "ghost" decor: Cut a banana in half and make a
  face by sticking three chocolate chips into the banana (two for
  the eyes, one for the mouth).

SPIDER BITES

SERVES **4 TO 6** PREP TIME: **20 MINUTES** COOK TIME: **15 MINUTES**

DAIRY-FREE, GLUTEN-FREE, NUT-FREE, VEGETARIAN

TOOLS TO GATHER

Cutting board

Chef's knife

Baking sheet

Wide spatula

Colander

Mixing bowls

Measuring spoons

Pastry brush

Spoon

Potato masher or fork

INGREDIENTS TO HAVE

2 tablespoons **olive oil**, divided

1 **large sweet potato**

¾ teaspoon **ground cumin**, divided

¼ teaspoon **salt**, divided

18 **pitted black olives**

1 **ripe avocado**

1 **lime**

These spider bites are delicious, not deadly! They're actually baked sweet potato slices topped with tasty guacamole and black olive "spiders."

1. **Preheat the oven, prepare the pan.** Preheat the oven to 425°F. Pour 1 tablespoon olive oil onto the baking sheet, then use the pastry brush (or paper towel) to coat the pan with oil.

2. **Slice the sweet potato.** Cut off the skinny ends of the potato. Slice the potato into rounds about ¼ inch thick. Place the 12 biggest slices on the baking sheet, discard the rest.

3. **Make the potato seasoning.** In a small bowl, add 1 tablespoon olive oil, ¼ teaspoon cumin, and ⅛ teaspoon salt. Stir with the pastry brush, then paint the seasoned oil onto the top of the potato rounds.

4. **Bake.** Bake on the first side for 8 to 10 minutes (until golden brown), then take out of the oven. Flip each potato round with the wide spatula, then return to the oven for 5 minutes. Use the spatula to transfer to the serving plate to cool.

5. **Cut the olive spiders.** Meanwhile, drain and rinse the olives. Using the bridge grip, cut 6 olives in half hotdog-style. Set halves aside. For the remaining 12 olives: Cut in half lengthwise, then

slice each half into 4 to 5 skinny slivers. Use a tiny version of the claw grip, holding the olive with pointer and thumb finger, to slice.

6. **Make the guacamole.** Cut the avocado, remove the pit and skin, and add to the medium mixing bowl (see Cooking with Avocado, page 140). Add ½ teaspoon cumin, ⅛ teaspoon salt. Cut the lime in half and squeeze juice from both halves into the bowl. Use the potato masher to mash the avocado and spices until very smooth.

7. **Assemble the bites and serve.** Once the potato rounds have cooled for 2 to 3 minutes, scoop 1 teaspoon guacamole onto each bite. Decorate with olive spiders by placing one of the olive halves in the center of each bite to make the body. Press 4 olive slivers on each side of the body to make the legs.

8. **Serve.** Serve warm or at room temperature.

Make ahead: This recipe is extra tasty when the potatoes are still warm, but you can also store the bites in an airtight container for up to 1 day and serve at room temperature. Or, you can make the different recipe parts ahead of time and bake the potatoes and assemble right before the party. Slice the spider olive bodies and legs and store in airtight containers. Make the guacamole and store in the fridge (see Cooking with Avocado, page 140) until the party starts.

Cooking with Avocado

Avocado is the star ingredient in guacamole, featured in the Spider Bites recipe. It can be kind of tricky to cook with, but after reading this you'll be an avo-expert! Guacamole stands great alone, so serve as a party snack at other parties (to make sure you have enough, use half an avocado per party guest).

CUTTING AN AVOCADO

Avocados have a hard pit in the middle. Cut on one side until you feel the pit, then spin the avocado to keep cutting around the out-side. Then take one half in each hand and twist apart.

If the avocado is very ripe, you should be able to squeeze the half with the pit and it will fall out, or you can loosen it with a spoon. To get the avocado flesh out of the skin, scoop it with a spoon. You can also use a butter knife to draw lines in the flesh going left to right and then up and down, and then scoop out the little cubes you've made—no need to dice!

KEEPING GUACAMOLE FROM BROWNING

When guacamole touches air for too long, it can turn brown and taste less yummy. One thing that helps slow down this process is adding lime to guacamole; that's one reason why most guacamole has lime (the other: It's delicious!). A second way to keep it from browning is to add a small amount of sour cream or Greek yogurt. Yet another way is to put your guacamole in an airtight storage container, then take plastic wrap and press it down until it touches the top of the guac. Put this container in the fridge. If it still browns, just scoop off the brown layer on top and eat the rest!

GRAVEYARD DIRT CUPS

SERVES 4 PREP TIME: 20 MINUTES CHILL TIME: 30 MINUTES

NUT-FREE, VEGETARIAN

TOOLS TO GATHER

Small saucepan

Dry measuring cups and spoons

Wooden spoon

Whisk

Flexible spatula

Gallon freezer bag

Juice glasses

Plastic wrap

INGREDIENTS TO HAVE

1 cup **pumpkin puree**

⅓ cup plus 2 teaspoons
maple syrup

1 teaspoon **pumpkin pie spice**

½ teaspoon **vanilla extract**

1½ cups **plain Greek yogurt**

3 **chocolate graham crackers**

Do you dare to dig up a graveyard? The delicious pumpkin mousse buried beneath the chocolate graham cracker "dirt" might give you the courage. Top each dessert cup with a graham tombstone, and for some gory flare, add gummy worms and candy eyeballs.

1. **Cook the pumpkin puree.** 🖐 In a small saucepan, combine pumpkin puree, maple syrup, pumpkin pie spice, and vanilla extract. Cook on the stove over low heat for 5 minutes, stirring occasionally.

2. **Add the yogurt.** Remove from the heat and let cool for 5 minutes. Add the Greek yogurt, then whisk to combine and make silky pumpkin mousse.

3. **Chill.** Use a flexible spatula to divide the pumpkin mousse evenly into 4 cups. Clean any messy mousse drips on the cup. Cover each cup with plastic wrap. Place in the fridge to chill for at least 30 minutes or up to 2 days.

CONTINUED

4. **Crumble the chocolate graham crackers.** Pour chocolate graham crackers into the gallon freezer bag. Crush with hands or smash with something heavy. Crackers can have large chunks, or you can smash until it's all fine "dirt."

5. **Decorate and serve.** Divide chocolate graham "dirt" on top of each pumpkin mousse cup. Decorate if you'd like (see decorating tip below). Set out cups on a serving platter. If they will be sitting out for a while, put ice cubes on the serving tray to help keep cups cold.

Decorate: Make this dessert extra spooky by making the cups look like a graveyard! To make edible tombstones, break 2 plain graham crackers in half so that you have 4 squares. Write "RIP" on each tombstone with a food coloring pen or gel icing. Stick the tombstone into mousse. If you have candy eyeballs or gummy worms, add 3 eyeballs and 2 gummy worms to each cup.

Monster Mash Freeze Dance

For this game, you just need a Halloween music playlist, speakers, and someone to play DJ. When the music is on, all players should dance like zombies or monsters. When the DJ presses pause, everyone must stop dancing. Whoever is the last to be moving when the music stops is out. Keep going until only a single zombie remains.

CHAPTER 14
Holiday Craft Fest

Invite your guests to come dashing through the snow to make awesome holiday crafts! Set the mood by playing holiday music, putting a Yule log video on the TV, and holding your party in a room near your holiday decorations. Secure your spot on the nice list with your festive snacks and crafty plans.

You can make and decorate the Gingerbread People (page 150) several days in advance, as long as you store them at room temperature in an airtight container after the icing dries. Prepare the Festive Hummus Pinwheels (page 148) the day before and assemble your pinwheel tree just before party time. Serve the pinwheels and any other snacks as guests arrive. Wait until dessert to whip up the Minty Hot Chocolate (page 146) and serve the Gingerbread People.

MINTY HOT CHOCOLATE

SERVES 6 PREP TIME: 10 MINUTES

GLUTEN-FREE, NUT-FREE, VEGETARIAN

TOOLS TO GATHER

Large stockpot
Measuring spoons and dry
  measuring cups
Whisk
Ladle (optional)

INGREDIENTS TO HAVE

½ gallon (8 cups) **milk** of choice
¼ cup **granulated sugar**
1⅓ cup **dark chocolate chips**
1 teaspoon **peppermint extract**

This hot chocolate uses milk (dairy, nut, or soy), real chocolate, and peppermint extract to bring that special warmth to your party. It's so easy, you can whip it up while your guests are crafting. Garnish with mini candy canes and marsh-mallows for extra holiday cheer.

1. **Bring the milk and sugar to boil.** Pour the milk into the large stockpot. Add the sugar to the stockpot and bring to boil over high heat. When the milk starts to boil, turn off the heat (it's okay if a skin forms on the top of the milk). Whisk to combine.

2. **Add the chocolate and peppermint.** Add the chocolate chips (or if using chocolate bars, break up first and then add). Whisk to combine. Add the peppermint extract, then whisk to combine.

3. **Serve.** Very carefully pour into 6 mugs. Remember to keep your non-pouring hand out of the way (don't hold the mug!) so you don't burn yourself if you spill. If it's easier, use a ladle to scoop the hot chocolate into mugs.

Swap it: If any of your guests don't drink regular milk, you can use almond milk, soymilk, or oat milk. If you can't find dairy-free chocolate, use dairy-free cocoa powder instead (about ½ cup, or more to your liking).

Holiday Snack-orations

Snack-orations means both snacks *and* decorations! Make a cheese wreath snack with cheese cubes, cherry or grape tomatoes, and ribbon. Arrange cheese cubes on a platter in a ring shape, place the tomatoes on top of the cheese. Tie a bow out of ribbon and place it at the bottom of the ring, and voilà! Cheese wreath snack-oration.

Make Santa hats with strawberries, bananas, mini marshmallows, and toothpicks. Cut the leafy ends off of the strawberries and slice the bananas into pieces ¼-inch thick. Slide a banana slice to the bottom of a toothpick, put a strawberry on top (flat edge on the banana), and top it with a mini marshmallow. These Santa snack-orations are sure to make you jolly.

FESTIVE HUMMUS PINWHEELS

SERVES 6 PREP TIME: 35 MINUTES

GLUTEN-FREE, NUT-FREE

TOOLS TO GATHER

Dry measuring cups and spoons
Colander
Food processor or blender
Cutting boards
Chef's knife
Flexible spatula
Toothpicks

INGREDIENTS TO HAVE

1 (14 ounce) can **chickpeas**
¼ cup **olive oil**
¼ cup **tahini paste**
½ teaspoon **salt**
1 clove **garlic**
1 **lemon**
2 **bell peppers**
6 10-inch burrito-sized **tortillas**
(spinach, if possible)
1 pound **sliced turkey**
12 slices **sliced cheese**

These protein-packed pinwheels will keep your guests spinning with enough energy to wait up for Saint Nick! They're filled with hummus, peppers, turkey, and cheese (or, leave out the meat to make them vegetarian). Arrange them like a tree with tomato ornaments for some extra holiday flair.

1. **Make the hummus.** Drain and rinse the chickpeas in the colander, then pour into the food processor (or a blender if you don't have a processor). Add the olive oil, tahini, and salt to the processor. Smash 1 garlic clove, peel, and add to the processor. Cut the lemon in half and squeeze the juice from both halves into the processor. Process until completely smooth.

2. **Cut the bell peppers, warm the wraps.** 🖐 Cut both bell peppers into strips about ½-inch wide. If tortilla wraps have been refrigerated, microwave for 30 seconds (this keeps the wraps from breaking).

3. **Assemble the wraps.** Place one tortilla on the second, clean cutting board. Scoop ¼ cup hummus (watch out for the blade!) and spread on the wrap with the flexible spatula, stopping about ½ inch from the edge of the wrap. Place 4 bell pepper strips on the edge closest to you. Place 2 slices of turkey on the hummus. Place 2 cheese slices on top of the turkey. Roll tortilla tightly around the bell peppers and keep rolling until the wrap is complete. Repeat for 6 wraps.

4. **Cut into pinwheels.** 🖐 With a sharp chef's knife, cut each wrap into sections about 1-inch wide. You should end up with 6 pinwheels from each wrap. Keep each piece from unraveling by poking a toothpick through the center of each pinwheel.

5. **Serve.** Keep the pinwheels refrigerated until serving, up to 24 hours.

Decorate: Make your pinwheels look like a tree waiting for presents to be put under it! Get a serving platter that's at least as big as a dinner plate. Make a circular layer of pinwheels on the bottom layer that's 12 to 14 pinwheels total (8 to 9 on the outside of the circle and the rest to fill it in). Make another layer on top that's a little bit smaller, and another layer that's a little bit smaller than that. The fourth level should be about 2 pinwheels, and the top only 1. For the tree topper, cut a star out of yellow paper, tape to a toothpick, and stick it on the top pinwheel. To make "ornaments," stick grape or cherry tomatoes on toothpicks and tuck them into the tree in between pinwheels.

GINGERBREAD PEOPLE

MAKES 12 COOKIES PREP TIME: 25 MINUTES
COOK TIME: 10 MINUTES CHILL TIME: 1 HOUR

NUT-FREE, VEGETARIAN

TOOLS TO GATHER

Mixing bowls

Measuring cups and spoons

Whisk

Electric mixer or stand mixer

Spoon

Flexible spatula

Plastic wrap

Rolling pin

3-inch gingerbread people cookie
  cutters (or other holiday shapes)

Wide spatula

Baking sheet

Nonstick spray

Cooling rack

INGREDIENTS TO HAVE

1 cup plus 2 tablespoons
  all-purpose flour

1½ teaspoons **ground cinnamon**

1½ teaspoons **ground ginger**

½ teaspoon **ground cloves**

¼ teaspoon **baking soda**

⅛ teaspoon **salt**

2 packed tablespoons
  brown sugar

¼ cup (half stick) **unsalted butter**

1 **egg yolk**

3 tablespoons
  unsulfured molasses

½ teaspoon **vanilla extract**

Gingerbread cookies not only are yummy, but also make your whole house smell like the holidays! Use gingerbread-people-shaped cookie cutters or other holiday themed cutters like stars, candy canes, or snowflakes. Leave cookies plain or decorate with a simple confectioner's sugar icing!

1. **Mix the dry ingredients.** In a medium mixing bowl, combine the all-purpose flour, cinnamon, ginger, cloves, baking soda, and salt. Whisk to combine.

2. **Cream the butter and sugar.** In a large mixing bowl, combine the brown sugar and softened butter (microwave butter for about 10 seconds if coming right from the fridge). Use an electric mixer or stand mixer to cream the butter and sugar together.

3. **Beat the wet ingredients.** Separate the egg yolk from the white over a small bowl. Pour the yolk into the large mixing bowl with the butter and sugar, then discard the white. Add the molasses, using a spoon to scrape from the measuring spoon. Add vanilla extract. Beat with electric mixer.

4. **Combine the wet and dry ingredients.** Add the flour mixture to the wet ingredients a little at a time, beating thoroughly to combine each time you add more flour mixture. The mixture will look crumbly but will stick together when pinched.

5. **Shape the dough and chill.** Cut a long piece of plastic wrap about 2 feet long. With your hands, form the dough into a ball. Press the dough on the plastic wrap into a rectangle shape, then cover with another piece of plastic wrap. Refrigerate for at least 1 hour or up to 3 days.

6. **Preheat the oven, prepare the pan, cut out the cookies.** Preheat the oven to 350°F and spray the baking sheet with nonstick spray. Take the dough out of the fridge and leave in the plastic wrap. Use a rolling pin to roll the dough to about ⅛ inch thick and cut out 12 cookies. See Cookie Dough Like a Pro (page 152) for more.

7. **Bake and serve.** Carefully transfer to the prepared pan. Bake for 8 to 10 minutes; cookies will harden more when cooled. Let cool for 5 minutes, then transfer with wide spatula to cooling racks. Serve plain, with a dusting of confectioner's sugar, or decorated (see tip below).

Decorate: Decorate your cookies with a simple icing: In a medium bowl, mix 1 cup powdered sugar, 1 tablespoon milk, and ½ teaspoon vanilla extract. You want the icing to be pretty sticky, but you might need to add a few more splashes of milk until you can stir the icing easily. Transfer to a small sandwich bag with a slider seal and cut a tiny bit from the corner of the bag. Squeeze icing out of the hole to add your designs to the cookies.

Cookie Dough Like a Pro

When you're making cookies with cookie cutters (instead of ones where you just plop a ball of batter on the cookie sheet), these tips will help them look great.

CHILL THE DOUGH

Chilling the dough helps cookies keep their shape better. It also makes it easier to cut the cookies out with cookie cutters. Here's how: First, cut a two-foot-long piece of plastic wrap and place on the counter. Next, form your dough into a ball, then place it on the middle of the plastic wrap and smoosh down. Shape it into a rectangle going in the same direction as your plastic wrap. Cut another piece of plastic wrap the same length and put it on top. Refrigerate for at least an hour, or up to three days in the fridge in an airtight container.

ROLL THE DOUGH

When the dough has been chilled for at least an hour, take it out of the fridge. Put it on the counter still in the plastic wrap. Use a rolling pin to roll the dough between the two pieces of plastic wrap until it's about ⅛ inch thick. Try to make all parts of the dough the same thickness.

CUT YOUR COOKIES

Peel off the top layer of plastic wrap, set aside. Use your cookie cutter to punch as many cookies into the dough as you can. (If you don't have a cookie cutter, you can also draw shapes with a butter knife). Here's the secret to keeping them from breaking: Peel away the extra dough first, and *then* pick up the cookies and transfer them.

   With your hands, carefully peel up the cut cookies and transfer them onto a greased baking sheet. Now it's time to take the dough scraps and make more cookies! Roll them into a ball, then shape into a rectangle. Put the top plastic wrap piece back on top, then roll out again. Cut as many cookies as you can and place on the baking sheet.

Let It Snow

Dreaming of snow? Make snowflakes out of paper! Gather 8½-x-11-inch printer paper and scissors. To make the printer paper into a big triangle, take one corner and fold it to the opposite side of the paper. Flatten the crease, then cut off the extra where the paper doesn't overlap. (You can also make snowflakes out of coffee filters.)

Fold it again, point to point, making a smaller triangle.

Cut shapes into all three edges of the triangle. Try half circles, squares, triangles, half hearts, or whatever you'd like.

Carefully unfold, and you'll have a snowflake! Repeat as many times as you'd like to make a blizzard!

These snowflakes make great window decorations; just tape to the window with clear tape. To make your snowflake sparkly, put craft glue on your snowflake and sprinkle glitter on top. To turn it into an ornament: Thread ribbon or yarn through one of the holes and tie.

MEASUREMENT CONVERSIONS

	US STANDARD	US STANDARD (OUNCES)	METRIC (APPROXIMATE)
VOLUME EQUIVALENTS (LIQUID)	2 tablespoons	1 fl. oz.	30 mL
	¼ cup	2 fl. oz.	60 mL
	½ cup	4 fl. oz.	120 mL
	1 cup	8 fl. oz.	240 mL
	1½ cups	12 fl. oz.	355 mL
	2 cups or 1 pint	16 fl. oz.	475 mL
	4 cups or 1 quart	32 fl. oz.	1 L
	1 gallon	128 fl. oz.	4 L
VOLUME EQUIVALENTS (DRY)	⅛ teaspoon	–	0.5 mL
	¼ teaspoon	–	1 mL
	½ teaspoon	–	2 mL
	¾ teaspoon	–	4 mL
	1 teaspoon	–	5 mL
	1 tablespoon	–	15 mL
	¼ cup	–	59 mL
	⅓ cup	–	79 mL
	½ cup	–	118 mL
	⅔ cup	–	156 mL
	¾ cup	–	177 mL
	1 cup	–	235 mL
	2 cups or 1 pint	–	475 mL
	3 cups	–	700 mL
	4 cups or 1 quart	–	1 L
	½ gallon	–	2 L
	1 gallon	–	4 L
WEIGHT EQUIVALENTS	½ ounce	–	15 g
	1 ounce	–	30 g
	2 ounces	–	60 g
	4 ounces	–	115 g
	8 ounces	–	225 g
	12 ounces	–	340 g
	16 ounces or 1 pound	–	455 g

	FAHRENHEIT (F)	CELSIUS (C) (APPROXIMATE)
OVEN TEMPERATURES	250°F	120°F
	300°F	150°C
	325°F	180°C
	375°F	190°C
	400°F	200°C
	425°F	220°C
	450°F	230°C

INDEX

ACKNOWLEDGMENTS

Thank you to Lauren Ladoceour, Vanessa Putt, and the team at Callisto Media for making this project a reality.

Thank you to the Stanford Learning, Design and Technology program for giving me the tools to explore cooking with kids and the encouragement to keep going. Thanks to Jamie Krenn, Ashley Smith, and Nomster recipe testers for making me a better recipe writer.

Thank you to my parents for supporting me every step of the way, Dan for making it possible for me to follow creative pursuits, and Juniper for inspiring me to say yes to hard things. Thanks to all the family, friends, and colleagues who have cheered me on, and to Jim for gifting me a lifelong love of cooking.

ABOUT THE AUTHOR

Ashley Moulton is the founder and Nomster-in-Chief at Nomster Chef (www.nomsterchef.com), a website that teaches kids to cook and love healthy food. She has worked in children's media for more than a decade at companies such as Nickelodeon, YouTube, and Google. She graduated from Stanford's Graduate School of Education with an M.A. in Learning, Design and Technology in 2015, and from Ithaca College as a Park Scholar with a B.S. in Television-Radio in 2009. Ashley's been an avid home cook and foodie ever since moving to New York City opened her eyes to the wonders of food, and hopes to share this love with as many kids as possible! She lives in Brooklyn with her husband and daughter. www.ashleymoulton.com

CPSIA information can be obtained
at www.ICGtesting.com
Printed in the USA
BVHW021313041219
565504BV00002BA/2/P